£7·95

ZAIRE

Christa Mang

GW00708146

BRADT PUBLICATIONS, UK
HUNTER PUBLISHING, USA

First published in English in 1991 by Bradt Publications, 41 Nortoft Rd, Chalfont St. Peter, Bucks, SL9 OLA, England from the German original by Conrad Stein Verlag, Kiel.
Distributed in the USA by Hunter Publishing Inc.

ISBN 0-946983-51-8

Translated from the German by Carrie Lynn Moulton
Photographs by the author
Maps by Gunda Siebke

FOREWORD

Since this travel guide is dedicated to my country, I gladly volunteered to write the foreword. I wish to express my thanks to Ms. Mang, who has rendered a remarkable service.

In the heart of Africa lies a subcontinent, a country of great geological variety and natural beauty rich in mineral resources: Zaire, my home.

The country surrounds the great Zaire river whose mass of water irrigates a huge valley basin far beyond the borders of Zaire. The boundless forest, the hot, oppressive sun, the grandiose storms, will impress you like a newly heard secret.

The love of life and the hospitality of the inhabitants will delight the patient and inquisitive traveller. Listen to Zaire's old traditional stories retold by an African. Rediscover man's roots and origins for yourself. Be prepared for something new and unique every step of the way. As with all populations of mixed ethnic backgrounds, the people are creative and resourceful, yet many tend to avoid difficult decisions. For a visitor this may be hard to understand; whatever your feelings, whether negative or positive, there is no room for indifference towards the country and its people.

A traveller can forget modern-day stress and leave worries behind. Though the road will be dusty, sometimes muddy, and often uncomfortable, wonder at the powerful river as it passes huge tropical forests and untouched savanna. Simply take in the beauty of nature. A wealth of events, landscape and emotions are waiting to be discovered.

The purpose of this publication is to be a realistic and practical guide to this immense country. The author, an objective observer devoid of prejudice and superfluous flattery, took upon herself to discover the country of Zaire by air, automobile and on foot. After reading this book or visiting Zaire you will have begun a relationship with my country, and I can guarantee that it will then be difficult to break away.

Mabolia Inengo Tra Bwato
Ambassador for Zaire in Bonn

PREFACE

This is Zaire: second largest country on the African continent, a land of contrasts, uniqueness and of natural wonders.

UNESCO gave the national parks of Virunga, Garamba and Kahuzi-Biega the title World's Cultural and Natural Inheritance. For me, the confrontation with mountain gorillas after a three-hour march through thick tropical forests high in the mountains was a touching experience of rediscovering a lost paradise.

Zaire is not a typical holiday country . There are no clubs here and no mass tourism, although Zaire is not lacking in good accommodation and sports facilities. One is not over-organized or burdened by choice. There is nothing superfluous.

You come to observe, to experience and gather impressions. Impressions of African village-life: lazy conversation under the mango trees, Mama stirring *fou-fou* at the hearth or baking *beignets*, African songs from morning to evening, the dull pounding of pestles in mortars, rhythmic tones here and there, the gentle stirring of unhurried life anchored fast to the laws of nature.

The people of Zaire are born cheerful, happy in the joy of life. One would gladly take some of this home.

Zaire is a country of contrasts, not just of landscape and climate, but culture. There is the contrast between modern, technocratic life and African tradition. A land of unfathomable mineral and agricultural wealth yet material poverty among the general population.

Development not only brings 'progress' it also produces chasms and separates, changes and destroys. The people of Zaire, fully aware of the situation, want, as their president once said, "... when scientists will have changed our living space Earth into an artificial environment, there will still remain Zaire, mankind's last refuge". Zaire is, incidentally, not a country of half-hearted compromises. It wants to be understood as it is.

There are a few pre-conditions required for a trip to this part of Africa. I wish to impart a piece of advice the ambassador of Zaire, His

Marabou stork in Vitshumbi fishing village

Excellency Mabolia, gave me, "Have a lot of patience." Patience alone, however, will not suffice. One also needs to be easy-going, tolerant, have a lot of time and a good sense of humour. Be adventurous and enthusiastic and be prepared to discover new and wonderful things.

Incidentally, you will rarely hear the forms of address Monsieur and Madame. One is addressed as Citoyen and Citoyenne and also in a respectful, friendly manner as Papa and Mama.

Have a pleasant trip!

Christa Mang
Le Tignet, December 1990

Merci - Thank You ...

... for the support in my work:
Cit. Commissaire Beyeye Djema - Minister for Culture, Art and Tourism, Kinshasa
His Excellency Mabolia and Mrs. Mabolia - Ambassador for Zaire in Bonn, Germany
Cit. PDG Botolo - General Director of the Federal Tourist Association, Kinshasa, Zaire
Cit. Dir. Ngimbi - Director of the Federal Tourist Association Kinshasa, Zaire
Viviane Ettlinger - Sales Representative for Air Zaire, Frankfurt, Germany
Prof. Gambembo and his family, Kinshasa
Alex Deprez - Director for Avis, Kinshasa
Rick Patterson - Avis, Lubumbashi

ABOUT THE AUTHOR

Christa Mang, with an educational background in commerce, has been working for 20 years in the tourist business (airline agency, travel coordinator, hotel management). She was recently employed as a travel guide at a German tour agency in southern France. Her native home is in Germany near Lake Constance, but since 1985 has been living in southern France near Grasse. Christa Mang's big interest is travelling independently. Her travel guide *Senegal* was likewise published by Conrad Stein in 1988, and in English by Bradt Publications.

Contents

PART 1

The Country

GEOGRAPHY

Zaire has a surface area of 2,345,000 km^2 and is the largest country on the continent after Algeria (2,376,000 km^2). The equator runs through the northern third of the country.

Zaire is surrounded by nine other countries: to the **north** lies the Republic of Congo, the Central African Republic and Sudan; to the **east** Uganda, Rwanda, Burundi and Tanzania; to the **south**, Zambia and Angola. The border measures 9,165 km. Zaire has a western gateway to the Atlantic along a 40 km coastal strip.

The tropical rain forest stretches across the equator like a saddle. Steppe-like plateaux, with elevations no higher than 400 m, cover the area from the Congo Valley in the west toward the east and south.

The coastal region in the southwest leans against the 1,000 m high mountain of the Crystal Massif. The Kasai Highlands stretch across the south, through which a net of rivers flow. Adjoined to the highlands is the Shaba Massif, earlier called the Katanga Highlands. A mighty mountain chain, approximately 50 km broad and 1,000 km long, runs along the country's eastern border.

The Mitumba Massif in the south, stretches across from Shaba into Kivu. The connecting Virunga mountain chain gave rise to a series of volcanoes, two of which are still active, Nyragongo (3,471 m) and Nyamulagira (3,056 m). The highest elevation in the Virunga Massif is the 5,119 m high Ruwenzori, the third highest mountain in Africa (Kenya 5,194 m and Kilimanjaro 5,895 m).

Extending in the northern part of the country is the savanna-covered Uele Tableland.

FLORA AND FAUNA

Almost half of the country is wooded, and Zaire makes up 47% of the entire African forest. The evergreen tropical forest stretches across both sides of the equator.

The impenetrable thicket of ferns and other shade-loving plants provide a refuge for the animal world. Majestic palms tower above this green mass ensnared in a net of lianas. The rich, immense forest is also an attraction for industry. The exploitation of the timber, including rare wood, is the main source of revenue for Zaire's agricultural industry.

Cultivated eucalyptus and pines grow in the higher elevations. Above 2,500 m are bamboo forests, and in between heather, lobelias and diverse lichens.

The slopes are covered with enormous banana, coffee and tea plantations, especially in Kivu. In addition, there are manioc and maize fields, and market gardens just like in our part of the world with peas and beans and other kinds of vegetables and fruit. Kivu's balanced climate provides optimal growing conditions.

Hunting grounds, natural sanctuaries and national parks have been established for the protection of wild game from, above all, poachers.

There are seven national parks in Zaire:

Salonga:	3,600,000 ha, established 1970
Upemba:	1,000,000 ha, established 1939
Maiko:	1,000,000 ha, established 1970
Kundelungu:	937,000 ha, established 1970
Virunga:	800,000 ha, established 1925
Kahuzi-Biega:	600,000 ha, established 1970
Garamba:	500,000 ha, established 1938

The Salongo National Park is the largest in the world. It is the only native home of the pygmy chimpanzee.

Another rare species is the okapi, which lives in the dense rain forest and due to its elusive nature was only brought to our knowledge in the

Roads in Zaire

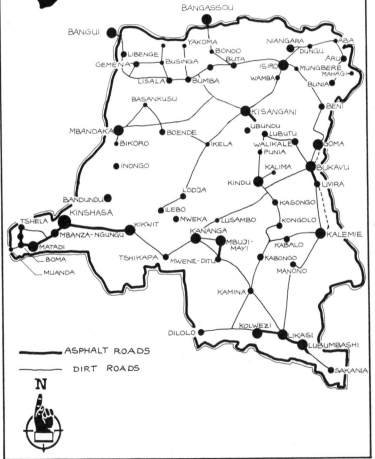

early part of the century. It survives today in Zaire. They are very shy animals but can be observed in the Epulu Reservation and the Ituri Forest.

In Garamba National Park live the black rhinoceros and giraffes in addition to the largest concentration of elephants in Zaire. In the savannas and forests are buffalo, hippopotamus (about 25,000), antelope, warthog, lion, leopard, baboon, etc. A large number of birds: pelicans, marabous, geese and birds of prey, among them eagles and vultures, abound throughout Zaire. Zaire's sanctuaries and parks offer an inexhaustible study field for all scientists.

The Institute Zairois pour la Conservation de la Nature (I.Z.C.N.), founded in 1969, is responsible for the administration and development of the national parks and natural sanctuaries. Kahuzi-Biega National Park is a Zairian-German coordinated conservation project in cooperation with the GTZ (Gesellschaft für Technische Zusammenarbeit - a cooperative association for technology).

HISTORICAL SURVEY

2,500 - 500 B.C.   Bantu (Bantu = man) tribes migrate to central Africa from the north. Various groups, the Lubas, Mongos and Bakongos, settled in western Zaire on the banks of the Congo river, in Kassai to the south and Lualaba to the southeast.

15th Century   The Congo Kingdom was established in the west from Gabon across Zaire south to Angola. The former capital Mbanza Congo is today's Sao Salvador in Angola. The Portuguese explored Africa's west coast and in 1482 Diego Cao discovered the mouth of the Congo River. The king of Congo, Nsinga-Nkuvu, established relations with Portugal and Spain. Portuguese settled in the country and Christianity was introduced in the Congo kingdom in 1491.

16th Century	The kingdom of Luba arose in the southeast (in Kasai and Shaba).
17th Century	The kingdoms of Kuba (in the northeast to the southwest) and Lunda (in the south to the southeast) arose. The Lunda established commercial relations with the Portuguese and Arabs and handled the slave trade.
18/19th Century	The kingdoms of Mangbetu and Zande were established in the north and northeast. In the south the M'Siri kingdom was established. Slave trade flourished. Slaves in groups of thousands were transported to Zanzibar and other central locations.
1850	Expeditions from Europe begin.
1866-1871	David Livingstone, the Scottish missionary and African explorer was searching for the source of the Nile. The western world lost contact with him and Stanley, a journalist with the New York Herald, was sent to look for him. They were up on the eastern shores of Lake Tanganyika.
1874-1877	Stanley explored the course of the Congo river. His discoveries were rebuffed by the British and offered to King Leopold II of Belgium who formed the International African (later Congo) Association to investigate the area.
1884-1908	The Association's rights to the Congo area were recognized at a Conference in Berlin and from 1885-1908 King Leopold and his agents exploited rubber and ivory (particularly) by methods which caused

an international scandal. Though roads and rail links were built the oppression of the people continued. Leopold finally relinquished control as a result of pressure from international critics.

10.18.1908

Leopold II ceded the country to Belgium. Multinational concerns establish themselves in Congo in order to exploit the mineral and agricultural resources and accelerate industrialization. The promotion to positions of higher responsibility still not possible for the African population.

1914 & 1940

Belgian Congo participated in both world wars on the Allies' side.

1955-1960

Rebellion spread in the country (Congo Crisis). Associations were started by former missionary students, political parties arose such as the ABAKO (Association of Bakongo) under the leadership of Kasa-Vubu and the MNC (Mouvement National Congolais) led by Lumumba. Appeals of Belgium's socialist party in favour of Congolese self-determination remained powerless; Joseph van Bilsen's plan for independence (1955/56) was rejected.

May 1960

Lumumba's party emerged as the strongest at the first parliamentary elections. Plans for cession were developed during Lumumba's government. Tschombé forms a one-party government (CONAKAT) in Katanga (today Shaba).

6.30.1960

In a situation of chaos and structural breakdown in the Congo Republic, the

16

country was proclaimed independent with the help of the Belgian king Baudoin I. Kasa-Vubu became State President, Lumumba became Prime Minister.

1960-1964

Bloody conflicts and separatist movements in the province Katanga (today Shaba) were first mitigated in 1963 by UNO intervention. Death of UN General Secretary Dag Hammarsskjöld (1961) in a plane crash whilst on his way to a peace talk in Katanga. General Mobutu took over the command of the army. Lumumba was murdered on 1.17.1961 during the course of the Katanga War. The circumstances of his death are still unknown today.

11.24.1965

President Kasa-Vubu is superseded by General Mobutu Sese Seko by a coup d'état. The general advocated peace and solidarity in the country.

1967

The party M.P.R. (Mouvement Popoulaire de la Révolution) was founded, and the currency zaire came into existence. On 5.20.1967 in his Manifesto of N'Sele Mobutu proclaimed a policy of Authenticity, striving toward economic independence and reflecting African cultural heritage. This Authenticity became the political maxim.

10.21.1971

The Congo Democratic Republic became Zaire with a new flag and new national hymn. The name of the river Congo was changed to Zaire.

2.15.1972

European names for towns, lakes, public establishments, etc. replaced by African

	names. (Leopoldville became Kinshasa, Elisabethville to Lubumbashi etc.)
11.30.1973	Establishment of a policy to give Zairian control to foreign businesses.
1975	Foreign businesses confiscated and the administration handed over to Zairians. Unfortunate mismanagement.
1976	60% of the asset value of the confiscated businesses were transferred back to former owners, who were compelled to take on a Zairian partner.
1977/78	Two invasion attempts into Shaba by the Congolese National Freedom Front were pushed back.
1980	In an anti-corruption campaign Mobutu decentralized public offices and undertook extensive government restructuring.
1982	A decree in February 1982 arranged for political representation in the eight provinces and in Kinshasa. Attempts in the spring to establish an official opposition party were forestalled.
July 1984	President Mobutu was reelected for another seven year term.
6.30.1985	25 years of independence.
11.24.1985	20th anniversary of the Second Republic.

POPULATION

The population of Zaire is 34 million. The average growth rate is approximately 3.1% annually, the mortality rate 16%. The average population density is 14 inhabitants per km^2. Zaire's population is young. The average life-expectancy is 52.5 years. Almost half of the population is employed with 13% in industry and mining, 76% in agriculture and 11% in the service sector.

The majority of inhabitants live in Kivu Province, following Kivu comes Haut-Zaire, Shaba, Bandundu with Kinshasa, Equateur, Kasai oriental, Kasai occidental and finally Bas-Zaire. Four main ethnic groups are distinguished in Zaire:

The **Bantus**, members of one of the largest tribes in Black Africa, make up almost half of the entire population in Zaire. They live dispersed in an area approximately two thirds of the country: from the north, to the border with the Central African Republic, to the southeast in Shaba.

The **Sudanese**, immigrants from the north who came between the 14th and 16th century, have settled mainly on the northern border between the rivers Ubangi and Uele.

The **Pygmies** are Zaire's oldest inhabitants. The word stems from the Greek *pygmaios* and means as big as a fist. The dwarf-size tribe (average size ca. 1.40 m or 4 ft. 6 ins.) number about 100,000 members.

They are exceptional hunters who are especially skilled in using poisonous arrows. Hunting is the main responsibility of the men, whilst the women collect fruit, leaves, snails, etc. for food and build huts out of twigs and foliage.

The Pygmies are monogamous and live in non-hierarchial family communities. Due to the clearing of the forest for timber, the Pygmies' living space has been drastically reduced. There are several Pygmy villages to be seen around Mont Hoyo

The Bambutis live mostly in the forests of the Ituri region in Haut-Zaire. Originally a nomadic people who lived exclusively in and from the tropical rain forest, they are today partially settled and integrated. In addition, the Nilotens and the Hamitens are settled in northeast and eastern Zaire. Other tribes in Zaire include the Baka, Babinga and the Batwa.

RELIGION

Half of Zaire's population is Catholic, 25% are Protestant, 1.5% Islamic, 3.5% Kimbanguismic and 20% belong to various other religious affiliations.

Kimbanguism originated in 1921 in Bas Zaire, 30 years following the birth of the prophet Simon Kimbangu. Kimbangu belonged to a baptist congregation (Baptist Mission Society, B.M.S.) and was a famous faith-healer. His following grew larger and larger, and a new religion, the Kimbanguistic church, began.

He was condemned to death in 1921 but then pardoned by the Belgian king, upon which he was deported to Katanga (today Shaba) and held prisoner for 30 years until 1951. In the mean time, Kimbanguism has become widespread making its way to Europe and the United States.

LANGUAGES

French is the official language in Zaire. Four main languages are spoken, and about 250 dialects.

Lingala:	In Kinshasa, Equateur, Haut-Zaire Lingala is also the military language.
Kiswahili:	In the eastern part of the country from Shabe to Kivu. Kiswahili is also one of the main languages in eastern Africa.
Kikonogo:	In Bas-Zaire and Bandundu.
Tshiluba:	In Kasai oriental and occidental.

FORM OF GOVERNMENT

Zaire is, according to the constitution of 1978, a social democratic centralized state. A one-party system is in existence, formed by the party MPR, Mouvement Populaire de la Revolution, founded in 1967. Every Zairian citizen is born a member of the party. All administrative authorities and institutions are accountable to the MPR. The president of the MPR, since 1965 Mobutu Sese Seko, is likewise the president of the republic.

The MPR Authorities

President of MPR, President of the Republic: He is the main authority for decision making and oversees the activities of the party. He is superintendent of all the MPR authorities. The President is elected by direct vote and serves a seven year term.

Congress (*le Congrès*): The Congress combines all the power figures of the nation. The method in which members of the Congress are appointed is decided by the Central Committee. The regular convention takes place every five years and is summoned by the President, although conventions can be summoned at any time. The main function of Congress is to decide on the doctrine of the MPR and on all issues dealing with the party's basic principles.

Central Committee (*le Comité Central*): Authoritative body for planning, suggestion, orientation and decision making of the MPR. The Central Committee makes sure MPR principles comply with the decisions made by Congress. Its members (membres du Comité Central) are appointed by the President and dismissed by him.

Politburo (*le Bureau Politique*): The Politburo supervises the decisions made by the Central Committee. Its members, the Ministers of State, are likewise appointed and dismissed by the President.

The Legislative Council (*le Conseil Législatif National*): The Legislative Council is made up of representatives (Commissaires du Peuple), who are elected by direct vote for a five year term.

The Executive Council (*le Conseil Executif National*): The Executive Council is composed of Ministers (*Commissaires d'Etat*). The first State Commissioner (= *Première Ministre*) has been Karl-I-Bond Nguza since 1980. The Ministers support the President (who is at the same time superintendent of the Executive Council) in national security affairs.

The Judicial Council (*le Conseil Judiciaire*): The Judicial Council comprises the highest Court of Justice, the general Council of Defense, the Court of Appeal, the Court of National Security. The administrative bodies of the individual regions and Kinshasa: The country is divided into eight departements (provinces) and Kinshasa. The regional government agencies are: the Regional Committee of the MPR, the Regional

Assembly and the Regional President of the MPR, and the State Governor. The Regional President is also the Mayor of Kinshasa.

The departements are further divided into sub-regions, rural communities, cities, etc., which in turn have their own administrations.

The President appoints and dismisses the Ministers and the top representatives in the government administration as well as the highest judges. Frequent restructuring of the Cabinet precludes power concentrations and prevents political alternatives outside the present administration. Attempts to establish an official opposition party have been forestalled up to this point. Unions, student and church groups have by and large integrated with the Mobutu regime, in other words they have adapted themselves. Nevertheless, an up-and-coming younger generation with a more critical stance toward the president and his authoritarian method of governing is making its way into the army, party and the government. A unified alternative to Mobutu's regime with ideas of real substance is, however, still in the making.

ECONOMY

Zaire is rich in mineral resources. Extending from Shaba, in the southeast of the country, to Zambia is the copper belt, from which above all copper, but also lead, zinc, silver, cobalt, cadmium, uranium and wolfram (from which tungstem is extracted) are mined.

In 1986 the country produced 505,258 t of copper, from which 452,200 t were exported. Zaire is the fifth largest copper producer in the world. Copper also brings in the most foreign currency for the country. Also mined is coal, natural gas is exploited , and since 1975, petroleum.

Zaire is number one in the world diamond market. In 1986, 23,303,739 carats of industrial diamond were produced, from which 23,233,000 carats were exported. Only a small portion is allocated for diamond jewelry. The diamond industry is located in Mbuji-Maji, in East Kasai.

The lumber industry represents the most important agricultural branch in Zaire. In 1986 the export quota was 123,064 m^3 from a total of 492,831 m^3 cleared (including rare ebony).

The coffee industry comes in second with 132,402 t (almost exclusively export), followed by palm oil with 105,726 t (20,384 t for export) and India ink with 14,165 t (export 12,588 t). The figures are likewise from 1986. In addition, manioc, bananas, sugar-cane, vegetables, peanuts, tea and cocoa are cultivated, mostly for consumption within the country.

About 20% of the entire agricultural land is used for farming, from which 70% of the population make a living. Because the annual inflation rate is very high (between 50 and 100%) and the resulting production costs too steep, the farmers cannot keep up and are therefore not very motivated to produce more than for their own needs. For this reason there is the tendency towards a subsistence economy. The distribution of agricultural produce is made difficult largely because of the huge distances and bad road conditions.

A few more statistics regarding tourism: In 1987 there were 36,167 foreign visitors in 1988, 39,444.

Time/Business Hours/Holidays
The country is divided in two time zones:

Kinshasa, Mbandaka, Matadi = Middle European Time (MEZ) - winter time - further east (Kananga etc.) = MEZ + 1 hour

Warning: The time change should be considered when booking flights. The respective local times are given.

Business hours for stores: Generally, Mon-Fri from 9.00-12.00 (in some cases 8) and 15.00-18.00, Sat. mornings, closed on Sundays.

Most of the restaurants are closed on Mondays.

Administrative offices and banks are open normally Mon-Fri from 8.00-14.30 or 15.00. The business hours for the post offices are generally Mon-Fri 7.30-12.00 and 13.00-16.30, and on Sat. 7.30-12.00.

Holidays
January 1	New Year's Day
January 4	Veterans' Day

May 1	Labour Day
May 20	Festival for the Party
June 24	Fishermen's Festival
June 30	Independence Day
August 1	Parents' Day
	Memorial Day
October 14	the President's birthday
	Youth Festival
October 27	Festival of the 3 Z's
	(when names Africanized)
November 17	Festival of the National Army
November 24	Day of the Second Republic
December 25	Christmas

Planning and Preparations

ARRIVAL

Via air
The airfare is relatively expensive. Further information available from travel agencies.

Flight connections within Africa
Air Zaire: on Sundays Kinshasa-Libreville-Luanda-Lomés-Abidjan-Conakry-Dakar; return on Mondays.
Air Gabun: on Fridays Kinshasa-Libreville-Kinshasa
Cameroon Airlines: on Tuesdays Duala-Kinshasa-Bujumbura-Nairobi; return on Wednesdays
Ethiopian Airlines: on Fridays Addis Ababa-Nairobi-Kinshasa-Abidjan; return on Saturdays

Air Afrique lands at Brazzaville in Congo. The ferry to Kinshasa can be taken from there.

Via ship
Two companies run ships between Zaire and Europe:

The Zairian *Compagnie Maritime Zairoise*(C.M.Z.) and the Belgian *Compagnie Maritime Belge* (C.M.B.) Both ships *Quellin* and *Kananga* run about once every two months between Antwerp and Matadi. (The *Quellin* also departs 9 days earlier from Hamburg). The trip lasts approximately 3 weeks with a week in port. The Belgian ship *Quellin* has cabins for 12 people. It is somewhat more comfortable than the *Kananga*. The *Kananga* can take 72 people (swimming pool on board). One-way fare for both ships with full board (88/89):

Antwerp-Matadi
A-Deck, 2-bed cabin, luxury category with shower/WC, zaire 85,000
B-Deck, 2-bed cabin, with shower/WC, zaire 73,000
C-Deck, 3-bed cabin, with shower/WC, zaire 60,000

Automobile up to 1700 ccm: zaire 20,000;   over 1700 ccm: upon inquiry.

Reservations should be made 3-4 months in advance. They book up rapidly especially during holidays. Information and reservations for both ships:

C.M.B. SA, St. Katelijnevest 61, B-2000 Antwerp, Tel. 03/2232418, 2232730, 2232353.

Via Automobile

The best-known road to Zaire is the Sahara crossing through Algeria, Niger, Nigeria, Cameroon, Gabon, Congo either through Central Africa or direct to Zaire. The best time for such a venture is the dry season, i.e. November until April. 4-wheel drive vehicles and good equipment are an absolute necessity.

The following are border crossings with neighbouring countries: Brazzaville (Congo), Mobayi and Zongo (Central Africa), Aba (Sudan), Mahagi, Kasindi and near Rutshuru (Uganda), Goma and near Bukavu (Rwanda), Uvira (Burundi), Sakania (Zambia), Dilolo, Tshikapa, Kahemba and Matadi (Angola).

Via Rail

From Zaire there are only railroad connections to the southern neighbours: from Lubumbashi through Dilolo to Lobito in Angola and from Lubumbashi through Sakania to Zambia, Zimbabwe and South Africa.

ENTRY REQUIREMENTS

Required for entry into Zaire are a valid passport, vaccination document and a visa. The International Vaccination Document must contain a record of immunization against yellow fever.

Visa applications can be requested from:

Embassy of the Republic of Zaire
26 Chesham Place
London SW1X 8HG

The applicant will receive four forms which should be sent back to the Zairian embassy along with the following supporting documents:

1. Valid passport with free pages
2. 4 passport photos
3. Travel documents
   a) for business trips: confirmation from the company (purpose of the trip, function of the traveller, confirmation of payment for round trip)
   b) for tourists: receipt from travel agency, medical certificate from family doctor stating that the applicant does not have any contagious diseases, International Vaccination Document (yellow fever). In addition, a customs voucher is required for entry with a motor vehicle. For a stay of over one month, police character certificate must be submitted.
4. To ensure reply, enclose a registered pre-paid self-addressed envelope.

Visa Fees

Transit with one entry: £ 9.00
Transit with multiple entries: £ 15.00
1 month with one entry: £ 18.00
1 month with multiple entries: £ 21.00
2 months with one entry: £ 27.00
2 months with multiple entries: £ 36.00
3 months with one entry: £ 45.00
3 months with multiple entries: £ 54.00

Visa takes about one week following submission of all supporting documents and payment.

MONEY

The currency is the **zaire**. It replaced the Congolese franc in 1967.

The following currencies in bills and traveller's cheques can be exchanged at all banks and larger hotels: English pound, German mark, Swiss franc, US dollar and Belgian franc. Private exchange is not officially permitted.

Travelling with US dollars is imperative. The admittance to all national parks, for instance, is payable only in US dollars. Dollars will also be accepted in hotels, travel agencies etc.

Nothing changes more rapidly in Zaire than prices. The prices given (89/90) are therefore only an approximation. Zaire is not an inexpensive travel destination. Here, as in other African countries, there are the local and the tourist establishments and prices reflect this. The tourist charges are comparable to European prices in hotels, restaurants, excursions, taxis at airports, etc.

The prices for a hotel room are generally posted at the reception desk. For most ordinary hotels the prices are determined per room and not per person. For a room in an average 2-star hotel one can expect to pay around £ 12-17. The prices in middle-class restaurants lie between £ 3-7.

CLIMATE AND TRAVELLING SEASONS

Zaire has various climatic zones and seasons. A warm, tropical climate with average temperatures throughout the year of 25° C is found on the **equator** and in **Kinshasa**. The humidity in the tropical forest is extremely high (up to 80%). The temperature remains constant between 30-35° Celsius and at night rarely falls below 20° C.

In **Bas-Zaire**, on the Atlantic coast, the average yearly temperature is about 26° C. In the high elevations of Kivu an almost Mediterranean climate is enjoyed throughout the year. The average yearly temperature here is about 20° C. The high plateaux of Kasai and Shaba have a similar climate. In the higher mountain regions of the Virunga Massif at an elevation of 2000 m, the temperature drops as low as 16-17° C, at 3000 m as low as 11° C, and at 4000 m to 6° C.

In the **north** between April and September, the prevailing winds come from the south, from October to March they are northerly. The *Alizé*, coming from the Indian Ocean, blows westwards throughout the year in the tropical region and from March to November in Shaba. Irregular northerlies blow from December until February. Southwest and westerly winds characterize the coastal region.

Seasons
South of the equator the rainy season lasts from October until April and the dry season from May until September. In addition, there is another short dry season in January.

North of the equator the times of the seasons are just the opposite.

In the higher mountain regions in the east it rains practically year-round, the only interruption being in July - the dry month. There is less rainfall from June to September and in January during the dry-season.

During the **rainy season**, brief but often very heavy rains alternate with clear, sunny weather. After a rainfall there is a rapid rise in temperature. On the coast and in Matadi it easily reaches 40° C.

The air is mostly clean and the skies blue at this time - perfect conditions for photographing. On the other hand, the unfavorable road conditions make it difficult to travel by automobile. Often the vehicle gets stuck in mud, and it is not uncommon for an entire stretch of road to be impassable.

During the **dry season**, cloudy skies and lower temperatures can be expected. This is the best time for travelling by car: the paths are very dusty yet passable everywhere.

For animal watching in the national parks, the conditions are generally more favorable in the dry season since during the rains the animals search cover in the forests.

Peak tourist seasons in Zaire are **summer holidays, Easter and Christmas**. Avoid these times if at all possible. Early booking of flights and excursions are advisable during peak seasons as well as reservations for hotels and visits to national parks.

Maps
Zaire, GUGK, 1:2.5 mill. (with geographical Index, map from USSR)
Republique du Zaire, Official Road Map, 1:3 mill.
Michelin Map Nr.955, Afrique Central et du Sud, 1:4 mill.

HEALTH

Vaccines
Immunization against yellow fever is obligatory for Zaire. Ask your family doctor. Immunization must take place no later than ten days before departure. The protection is effective for ten years. The

immunization should be registered in the vaccination document, which must be presented upon entry into Zaire. It might also be requested for air travel within Zaire.

Cholera vaccination is still recommended for travel to infected areas. Currently this is not the case for Zaire. This vaccination protects against only 40-50% of cases. Always be careful of what you eat and drink.

Tetanus and Poliomyelitis

Poliomyelitis protection is given to all children in the UK - adults should have a booster before travelling overseas. Tetanus is also recommended.

Hepatitis-A

The hepatitis-A virus, like the cholera virus, is almost exclusively transmitted by means of food or liquid intake. For this reason it is especially important to observe basic hygiene rules. An intra-muscular vaccine immunizes for three to six months.

Hepatitis-B

The hepatitis-B virus is transmitted the same way as the HIV virus, i.e. via sexual contact with an infected person or contact with infected blood. The hepatitis-B immunization course must be started four months before departure since it only begins to take effect after three vaccinations. The vaccinations are given at intervals of one a month and the vaccination should be repeated after one year.

Typhus

The virus is transmitted orally, through food and liquid intake (therefore be careful when drinking water, ice cubes, ice cream). Appropriate protective measures are strongly advised here. An oral vaccine should be completed no later than one week before departure date. Immunization lasts one year. Beware of side effects. Observe instructions carefully.

Malaria-Prophylaxis

This is indispensable since malaria is the most widespread disease in Zaire, as in most African countries. Malaria is transmitted mainly between sunset and sunrise via the female Anopheles mosquito. The virus (Plasmodium falciparum) has become Chloroquin resistant. For up to date advice on which prophylactic to take, ask your G.P. or phone the Malaria Reference Laboratory, London, tel. 071 636 7921. The course should be started three weeks before departure. Further precautions are:

1. Wearing bright clothes (long sleeves, trousers) in the evenings.
2. Mosquito protection on windows or take a self-standing mosquito net with you.
3. Applying insect repellent on exposed skin and spraying area with insecticide.

Running a high temperature is a symptom of malaria, in addition to nausea, vomiting, aching in back and limbs and dizziness. Take with you a supply of Fansidar or other malarial cure containing sulfonamide. Ask your doctor. The tablets are available in Zaire in the larger pharmacies and hospitals.

Bilharziosis
This life-threatening disease is caused by tiny worms which penetrate the skin and make their way into the bloodstream. Bilharzia must be treated immediately, otherwise it can be deadly.

Never step into stagnant water! Swimming in inland water is not recommended, but if you are tempted ask the local people if the disease is prevalent. Upon returning home be examined by a doctor if you have bowel irregularities or blood in the urine. There is no preventive vaccine against bilharzia, but it is cured by a single dose of Praziquantel.

AIDS
The ways by which the HIV virus is transmitted are commonly known. The appropriate precautions should be observed here as well. According to current scientific research, the HIV virus is not transmitted by insect bites. According to information from a number of physicians and institutions, blood donations in Zaire are tested for HIV. As a precaution, disposable syringes could be taken with you.

Tip: If a wound suddenly develops on the skin surface, it could have been caused by larvae. This is due to insects laying eggs in damp washing hung out to dry. Neba cetin or Graneodine (available in most pharmacies in Zaire) are a quick remedy.

As first-aid materials the following items are recommended: dressings (Bandaids and gauze), elastic bandages, pocket-size scissors, clinical thermometer, medication against diarrhoea and constipation, aspirin, disinfectant, antiseptic cream, eye-drops, antihistamine ointment for insect bites, insect repellent and medication for malaria.

Stock up on supplies of regularly taken medication at home, allergy control or cardiac stimulant, etc.

For immediate care go to a mission station or a village clinics. There are hospitals, European physicians and dentists in the larger cities. In extreme cases request to be transported to the Ngaliema hospital in Kinshasa. Make sure you have insurance coverage in case you need to return to Europe for emergency treatment. In case of emergency contact your embassy.

LUGGAGE

Often the question arises: Should I take a backpack? It is certainly practical, but tends to convey the image of the not too highly regarded backpack tourist.

An alternative is a suitcase-backpack. Very practical: with a few deft manoeuvres it can be altered from a backpack to a suitcase or shoulder bag. As lighter luggage there are also special travel shoulder bags. Make sure, however, that the strap is wide enough so that it does not dig into the shoulder while carrying.

Whether backpack or travel bag, the material should be made out of plastic not easily ripped and of good quality overall. Furthermore, the luggage should be made to lock. In case that it does not have locking capability, padlocks or suitcase locks can be used. For one-day excursions, a small backpack or shoulder bag is practical to take along necessary articles.

For a 4-week sojourn in Zaire, the following equipment is advisable:

1   Pair sturdy trainers
1   Pair open shoes (sandals)
1   Pair thongs (for use in community showers)

2   Pairs cotton trousers
1-2 Pairs cotton skirt or culottes
2-3 Pairs cotton socks
4-5 T-shirts
Cotton undergarments

1   Somewhat smarter dress/shoes for possible invitations, going out
1   Older trousers, shirt and trainers for gorilla-seeing and hikes in the
     forest (clothes will get dirty)
1   Cotton sweater with long sleeves or sweatshirt
1   Foldable rainwear
2   Towels
1   Hand-towel for on the road
1   Cotton sleeping-bag (see *Glossary*)

Toiletries (transfer to plastic containers)
Torch and spare battery
Pocket-knife and if necessary, camping gear
Insecticide (for skin application and spraying area)
A few empty plastic bags (for dirty washing etc.)
Toilet paper or tissues (transfer from bulky packaging to plastic bags)
Plenty of moist towelettes (possible gift articles)
Travel alarm
Medication (see *Health*)

This travel guide and additional map materials if needed
Notebooks (for tips, addresses and possibly as small gifts)
Supply of pens

Concentrated detergent in a tube
Travel clothes-line and pegs
Travel sewing-kit
Sunscreen, -glasses, -hat
Water bottle (1 litre)
Water-sterilizing tablets

Photo-equipment, film, spare batteries and aluminium film bags
Passport, vaccination document, traveller's cheques and cash
Photocopies of passport, checks and flight tickets (recommended; keep
separate from originals)

As small gifts: pens, pencils and coloured pencils, notebooks, simple necklaces, mini bars of soap, moist towelettes, Eau de Cologne, Bandaids, aspirin, pocket mirrors and knives, T-shirts with print (or leave behind clothes worn which are no longer needed).

Pack clothes in separate plastic bags, leaving enough room for air to circulate. The electric current in Zaire is 220 V A.C.

CUSTOMS

According to the Washington Convention (CITES), the following import restrictions apply to Great Britain:

The importation of the skins of predatory animals, ivory, living or stuffed birds, tortoise-shell or tortoises, crocodile purses or snake skins, shells, cactuses, orchids or other wild plants not commercially grown are forbidden. Special permission for the export and import of certain objects is required.

In Zaire

TRAVELLING IN THE COUNTRY

One can travel in Zaire starting from Kinshasa with an organized tour or independently. There are also tour operators who offer excursions to Zaire from Rwanda and Burundi.

In Kinshasa there are quite a few travel agencies who offer excursions. The organized excursions specialize mainly in the following: **Kivu** (Virunga National Park, animal safaris, observation of mountain gorillas, the villages Goma and Bukavu), Lubumbashi/Shaba (Kundelungu and l'Upemba National Parks, animal safaris, visit to copper industry).

The animal safaris from Lubumbashi are conducted by Avis in coordination with Air Zaire and the hotel Sheraton Karavia. Generally a minimum participation of four or more people is required for the excursions. Special arrangements are possible, however the prices for only one to two participants are astronomical. The group prices alone for the excursions are already exorbitant.

Considering, however, the enormous total expenditure of the trips with accommodation generally in the best, most expensive hotels and the relatively steep admission fees for the national parks, the high prices for the excursions are then understandable.

The list of interesting places in Zaire continues: for example the Wagenia Fishery in Kisangani, the Okapi Sanctuary Epulu, Lakes Mukamba and Fwa, Gungu's Cultural Festival, the Salonga National Park, Matadi and Bas Zaire, Lakes Tumba and Mai Ndombe, Lake Tanganyika, not to mention the as yet undiscovered secrets.

Mobility is a problem in many places in Zaire, i.e., a challenging part of one's travel adventures. Travelling independently requires sufficient time, agility and fitness to endure long waiting, extreme climatic conditions (heat, high humidity), travelling on rough roads, long hikes or whatever the case may be. Furthermore, one should have a generous travelling budget. Zaire is not the place for cheap tourism.

The distances are immense in Zaire: 2,900 km from Kinshasa to Lubumbashi and 2,600 km from Kinshasa to Goma. The metropolis is not situated in the centre but quite far over to the west.

Travelling by air is the best way to conquer such distances. Zaire's air network is well developed, however it is not uncommon that departure times are delayed and flights cancelled at short notice. Flexibility and sufficient time are helpful in such situations, so that delays in one's trip are of little consequence.

In the heart of the country the roads, even the main stretches, are still largely compact earth. Exceptions are the stretches Kinshasa-Matadi-Boma, Kinshasa-Kikwit, Lubumbashi-Kolwezi as well as several kilometres between Kisangani and Bukavu.

Projects for further construction of national roads are planned. A few of them are soon to be put into action, for instance the section Kikwit-Kolwezi, the main stretch connecting Boma/Matadi/Sakania (the coast to the Zambian border). A complete redevelopment of the stretches Kisangani-Bukavu and from Kisangani further north through Buta to the Central African Republic border (Bangassou) are also planned. This stretch, starting from Kivu, will make up part of the Transafrica-Route connecting Kenya with Nigeria.

Running through Kivu is the *Route de la beauté*, which does credit to its name during the dry season but reverts to muddy ruts during the rains. Nevertheless it is hard to imagine this road paved. Certainly it would lose its adventurous charm.

Due to the lack of public transport in Kivu, renting a car is recommended, especially for the north of Goma. It is a worthwhile experience and with a group of people more economical (see *Travelling in Kivu*). Also worthwhile is a trip by train, from Kinshasa to Matadi with the Express rail or a short excursion from Kisangani to Ubundu. If one allows enough time to wait one to several days for transport, whether it be truck, ship, airline or rail, then mobililty is by all means manageable-and travel adventure is guaranteed.

Be communicative, since this is the way to learn many useful pieces of information. The Zairians are very open-minded and talkative.

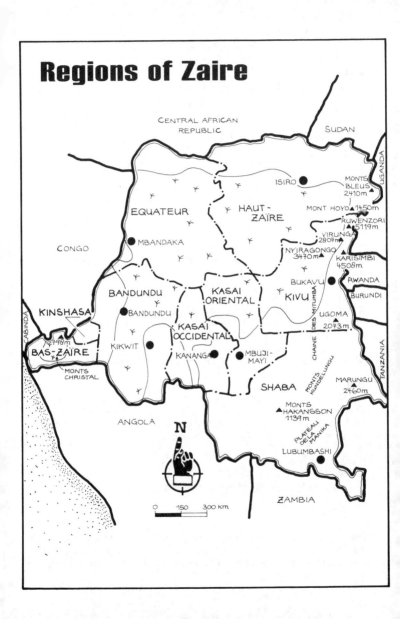

Regions of Zaire

CENTRAL AFRICAN REPUBLIC

SUDAN

UGANDA

ISIRO

MONTS BLEUS 2410m

MONT HOYO 1450m

EQUATEUR

HAUT-ZAÏRE

RUWENZORI 5119m

VIRUNGA 2807m

CONGO

MBANDAKA

NYIRAGONGO 3470m

KARISIMBI 4508m

BUKAVU

RWANDA

BANDUNDU

KASAI ORIENTAL

KIVU

BURUNDI

KINSHASA

BANDUNDU

UGOMA 2073m

BAS-ZAÏRE

~798m

KIKWIT

KASAI OCCIDENTAL

KANANGA

MBUJI-MAYI

TANZANIA

MONTS CHRISTAL

SHABA

MARUNGU 2460m

MONTS HAKANSSON 1139m

ANGOLA

PLATEAU DE LA MANIKA

LUBUMBASHI

N

ZAMBIA

0   150   300 km

Rail

Zaire has a railway network approximately 4,600 km long. Rail transportation is under the supervision of S.N.C.Z. (Société Nationale of Chemins de fer Zairois). The following railway lines are in existence:

in the **north**: Bumba-Aketi-Buta-Isiro-Mungbere Kinsangani-Ubundu
in the **south and southeast**: Lubumbashi-Sakania (Zambian border)
     Lubumbashi-Likasi-Kolwezi-Dilolo (Angolan border)
     Lubumbashi-Lakasi-Kamina-Kabalo-Kalemie
     Lubumbashi-Likasi-Kamina-Kabalo-Kongolo-Kasongo-Kindu
     Lubumbashi-Kikasi-Kamina-Kanaga-Mweka-Ilebo
in the **southwest**: Kinshasa-Mbanza-Ngungu-Matadi

Ship

The Zaire and Kasai rivers and their tributaries make up a transport net of approximately 14,500 km. In addition, shipping lines on the lakes make up about 1,300 km. The main lines are:

Kinshasa-Ilebo (on the Zaire and Kasani rivers)
Kishasa-Mbandaka-Kasangani (on the Zaire)
Moba-Kalemie-Uvira (on Lake Tanganyika)
Bukavu-Goma (on Lake Kivu)

Shipping traffic is run by the ONTRA (National Office of Transport).

Bus

Smaller enterprises, mainly the two companies Sotraz (Société de Transport Zairois) and Sitaz, share control over the buses in Zaire. For the most part the buses are comfortable and each person is guaranteed a seat. The following lines have been established:

Kinshasa-Matadi (daily)
Kinshasa-Kikwit (daily)
Lubumbashi-Likasi-Kolwesi (several times daily)

SHOPPING

One can buy many souvenirs: masks, wooden carvings, malachite jewelry and other objects made from this material, pictures, copper reliefs, ceramics, purses and mats woven from palm leaves, precious

Train and Airline Connections

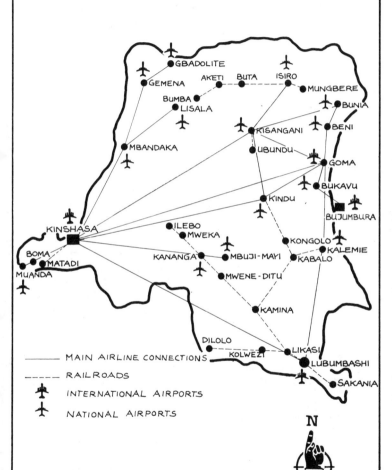

GBADOLITE
GEMENA
AKETI   BUTA   ISIRO   MUNGBERE
BUMBA
LISALA   BUNIA
BENI
KISANGANI
MBANDAKA   UBUNDU   GOMA
BUKAVU
KINDU   BUJUMBURA
KINSHASA   ILEBO
MWEKA   KONGOLO
BOMA   KANANGA   MBUJI-MAYI   KALEMIE
MATADI   KABALO
MUANDA   MWENE-DITU

KAMINA

DILOLO   LIKASI
KOLWEZI   LUBUMBASHI
SAKANIA

─────── MAIN AIRLINE CONNECTIONS
- - - - - RAILROADS
✈ INTERNATIONAL AIRPORTS
✈ NATIONAL AIRPORTS

N

stones, imaginative toys for children made out of copper and iron wire, splendid, colourful cotton material amongst many other items.

The largest and most significant arts and crafts market is the *marché de l'ivoire* (ivory market). Please don't be tempted to buy ivory - there are many other beautiful souvenirs for sale. Here the prices are *à discuter* (open for bargaining). Bargaining is a supreme law in the tourist market! Inquire about the price then suggest half of it. Be patient. Let the seller do the suggesting, your reaction only "c'est trop cher" (that's too expensive), hesitate, smile, move away slowly ...

If you yourself suggest a price, you are obliged to pay that much. It is an established rule. You cannot bargain it any lower. Generally bargaining is only for souvenirs, not appropriate at the daily or weekly public markets (unless you think you are being over charged).

Souvenirs can also be bought in front of the tourist hotels (for example in the Karibu and Masque hotels in Goma). Both of the souvenir shops in Goma (see *Goma*) offer a wide variety of jewelry, pottery and basket ware.

The best place for copper reliefs is at the brothers' Chenge in Lubumbashi. The best paintings and water colours by Zairian artists are found in Kinshasa and Lubumbashi. In the national museum in Kinshasa there is a selection of works of art for sale. Ask here for more information on artists or inquire at the Cultural Institutions in both cities.

The bright, beautifully patterned cotton material is found most reasonably priced at the *grand marché* in Kinshasa or in the shops under the arcades in Kisangani. In Kinshasa there are a few wholesalers who occasionally sell to individuals. Your best bet is to ask a Zairian woman for information.

For further information see *Customs*.

FOOD AND BEVERAGE

Almost everywhere, even in the smaller villages, international cuisine is served. In the cities of Kinshasa and Lubumbashi the range extends from snackbars to pizzerias, Chinese restaurants to nouvelle cuisine, and likewise no shortage of exclusive restaurants.

The small, typical African restaurants offer local cuisine, however, so if native specialties are your desire ask a Zairian for tips.

The staple for Zairian cuisine is manioc. The roots and leaves of manioc are used. The oblong, white tubers have to be soaked in water a few days in order to draw out certain poisonous elements. Afterwards they are laid out to air-dry, then sold in the market in the dried form. The cook crushes the pieces in a mortar into flour, from which the Zairian main dish *fou-fou* (a Lingala word) is made.

There is hardly a housewife who does not serve her family *fou-fou* at least once a day. Generally it is a thick, chewy dumpling served with meat or fish with gravy. The dumpling is made by vigorously stirring the sifted flour little by little into boiling water, until the best consistency is achieved. Depending on the region *fou-fou* is made either solely from manioc flour (in Bas-Zaire and Bandundu) or mixed with maize flour (in Shaba).

Chikwange is a somewhat different form of *fou-fou*. Here the manioc batter is wrapped in leaves (mainly banana leaves) and then boiled. *Chikwange* is above all provision for the road. *Saka-saka* is prepared from manioc leaves and is similar to spinach.

The Zairian specialty *mwambe* (or *moamba*), consists of chicken in a hot palm oil sauce, sometimes mixed with crushed peanuts.

Sweet potatoes and dried cooking bananas are also puréed and served with meat or fish dishes. Zairians generally eat a lot of meat and fish. Besides goat, pork, rabbit and beef, wild game is especially esteemed, for instance antelope, buffalo and monkey among others.

Among fish types there are capitaine or Nile perch and several Tilapia species. *Liboke* is a specialty of fresh water sadine prepared in a typically African manner by fishermen's wives in Maluku and Kinkole.

Pili-pili, or hot pepper is, incidentally, hardly ever missing from a Zairian dish.

As for cereals, rice, corn and millet are most common. In the higher elevation (e.g. Kivu), where beans, peas and carrots are cultivated, the diet is richer in vegetables.

A large variety of exotic fruits grow here such as various sorts of bananas, pineapple, mangos, mangosteens, lichees, maracujas (passion fruit) and guavas.

Drying, smoking and scorching the skin are the methods used to preserve fish and meat. For the most part, thoroughly cooked meat and fish can be eaten without concern. Uncooked vegetables and fruit (the latter preserved by nature in its protective wrapping) should be washed with purified water.

Caution: Consumption of damaged or cut fruit and vegetables should be avoided. Likewise ice-cream (see *Health*).

The Zairian national beverage is beer. There is quite a variety of brands produced by a large number of brewers. Water or soft drinks may not be available in some cases, but beer is always to be found.

Freshly squeezed fruit juices, above all marcuja juice, are offered in most of the larger hotels and restaurants. Likewise coffee and tea are available most everywhere. In the better, more exclusive restaurants one can order French wines. The villager's favourite beverage is palm or banana wine. Powdered or diluted canned milk take the place of fresh milk as a rule.

PHOTOGRAPHY

The amateur photographer will be confronted with many varied conditions. The uninhibitedness and openness of the villagers are often just the pre-requisites for capturing everyday impressions, especially in the remote African villages.

Nevertheless, one should not walk around with a camera around the neck ready for a quick shot upon spotting potential prey. Discretion and consideration, especially in villages still to a large extent untouched by the modern world, should be a matter of course. If possible, try to start a conversation with the villagers before casually taking their picture.

Always ask permission before photographing someone. It is also advisable to ask the head man of smaller villages (if he is to be found) for permission to take pictures.

Be flexible if the whole family insists on lining up before the camera for a group shot. Afterwards you can take a few snapshots of your choice.

Occasionally money or a present may be requested for taking someone's picture. Paying money does not seem appropriate to me. Instead I think it better to promise to send copies as a memento (but stick to that promise). Pens (Bic's) for children, cigarettes for the fishermen perhaps, and for the mothers a few aromatic decorative soaps, moist towelettes or Bandaids are likewise appropriate.

Taking pictures at the open markets can cause more significant problems. One is not too infrequently confronted with complete refusal when attempting to shoot at random. Ask permission first from someone or, if possible, from the person in charge there. Nevertheless, the best way is to start talking with a market woman, buy something from her and express rather casually that you want to take a picture. Then you will rarely be refused.

Warning: It is **prohibited** to take pictures of military establishments or public buildings, e.g. airports and harbours, bridges, train stations, city halls, government and administrative buildings, etc. as elsewhere in Africa. Disregarding this rule could lead to the confiscation of the film or even the camera.

WATERWAYS

The mighty Zaire River (formerly the Congo) makes a wide sweep through the country westward and has many tributaries. The word *Zaire* means 'the large river'. The Zaire, measuring 4,640 km long, is the fifth longest in the world. As for the mass of water transported, the Zaire ranks second, (after the Amazon) with 40,000 m^3 per second.

The river arises as the Lualaba in Musofi, a village with an elevation of 1,435 m in the Shaba district, not far from the Zambian border. The Lualaba flows to Kisangani and is only partially navigable.

From Kinsangani, it then continues as the Zaire through the tropical rain forest. South of Mbandaka it forms the border with the Republic of Congo. After 1,734 km it reaches Kinshasa. The entire stretch from Kisangani to Kinshasa is navigable.

The stretch from Kinshasa to Matadi is unnavigable due to several dangerous rapids of 265 m to 300 m. One of the most powerful with a drop from 102 m to 15 m above sea level has been utilized to build one of the largest dams in the world. Upon completion of its third and last stage of construction, INGA, the hydroelectric power station erected here, has become the most powerful in all of Africa. (see *Matadi*)

The Zaire and its tributaries serve not only as a major energy source, but with 14,166 km of navigable waterways they are also very important transportation channels.

The land is strewn with impressive waterfalls, of which the 384 m high Lofoi, located in Kundelungu National Park, is the highest in Africa.

Of a total of approximately 15 lakes, Lake Tanganyika is the deepest (1,470 m) in the world next to Lake Baikal. Lake Kivu lies at an elevation of 1,400 m, the highest elevation of all lakes in Africa.

MAIL/TELEPHONE/TELEX

Postage
Letter to Europe: 10 g zaire 80, 15 g zaire 95, 20 g zaire 110
Postcard: (5 g) zaire 80

A letter overseas takes approximately 10 days, postcards longer. For quicker delivery send postcards in an envelope. Mail to Zaire is distributed only in post-office boxes (B.P. = Boite Postale). Mail can be sent poste restante to Kinshasa addressed in the following manner:

Name
Poste restante
ONPTZ
Kinshasa 1
Zaire

One can pick up letters, etc. at the counter upon presentation of passport. The same is valid for packages. It is easier to have mail sent to a private address.

Warning: If at all possible avoid sending urgent or valuable things by post. Mail is often lost.

Telephone

Within the country: Only Kinshasa and Lubumbashi can be dialed directly.

The dialing code for Kinshasa is 012, followed by the 5 digit number. Dialing code for Lubumbashi is 02, followed by the 6 digit number. Direct calls can be made only to these following countries outside Africa: Belgium, Spain, USA, UK, France, Greece, Switzerland and Germany.

First dial 00, then the respective country's dialing code (e.g. 0044 Britain), the area code (without a 0) and finally the number required.

Rate: 1,230 zaires per minute plus 18% tax. A minimum of 3 minutes are calculated = 4,358 zaires. There are no special rates.

Telex

Fee: 1 minute 1,100 zaire plus tax, minimum of 3 minutes = 3,945 zaire.

TIPS

In general, tips are handled no differently in Zaire than anywhere else. One should tip in a restaurant as well as for room service in a hotel. Furthermore, it is better to tip the maid personally if you know who it is (usually she introduces herself).

If you should forget to leave a tip, you can rest assured that in one way or another you will be reminded accordingly, even (and especially) when a tip, or cadeau, is not customary. If this is the case, bring this to their attention in an unmistakable yet friendly manner.

With services it is another story. If you accept a service, even one volunteered, it is generally expected that you show your gratitude by monetary means. As everyone knows, need creates inventive energy, and it is astonishing with what creative energy, especially the young Zairians, operate! Before you can turn around, someone is offering to help you at opportune as well as inopportune times. Remember, if no requests are made, there are no obligations.

This creativeness is nevertheless a relief if the automobile gets stuck somewhere with no help in sight. All of a sudden, as if fallen from the sky, assistants appear, and lend a hand without hesitation, as if they had never done anything else but dig cars out of the morass. Then this creativeness is definitely worth a few zaires!

Tip: It is a good idea to carry a few packs of cigarettes with you. Even given out individually they are very valuable small tokens of appreciation.

PART 2

Regional Guide

KINSHASA

The Zairian metropolis and Black Africa's largest city has currently 3.5 million inhabitants, making up over 10% of the entire population of the country. The city still has some room to expand in the south, and that itself seems to be a process without end. New residential areas are growing up like weeds.

The river Zaire forms the northern border of the city. Around the Zaire is a broad area where the river washes up on the shores of many small islands and sandbanks. These are favourite leisure spots for the inhabitants of Kinshasa (the Kinois) and for visitors to the city. On the opposite side of the river is Brazzaville, the capital city of the neighbouring country, the Republic of Congo.

Comparable to other metropolises, Kinshasa is a city of many contrasts. But here in Kinshasa the dimensions seem to be especially large. What perplexes the visitor is the coexistence of the African tradition and the modern, technocratic life. The more the one develops, the stronger the other seems to assert itself.

Directly from the airport one drives through the broad Boulevard Lumumba, lined with small African restaurants and pubs (buvettes), interspersed with small markets and eucalyptus groves and giant bill-boards, especially those of the party M.P.R. with the president's portrait.

Towering above the city, as if in salute to the modern Zaire, is a high, grey concrete tower (150 m); a useful landmark for the tourist. To the left of the tower is the residential district Lemba and beyond it the university, to the right the boulevard continues past the fair grounds FIKIN beyond Limete, one of the nicer residential areas in Kinshasa, to the centre of the city.

This is the beginning of the main traffic artery, the 5 km long Boulevard du 30 Juin, which passes through the heart of the city. Here, in the **Gombe** district, on the boulevard and in the side-streets, one can find almost everything of importance: banks, office buildings, travel agencies, businesses and shops, restaurants, etc. Shortly before the Boulevard du 30 Juin (often just Boulevard for short) runs into the Avenue du Colonel Mundjiba, the Batetela Avenue branches off to the right towards the river bank. The 5-star hotel Intercontinental is located there. Most of the embassies are also located in this district along with several clinics, among them the best, Clinique de Ngaliema.

The ivory market (*marché de l'ivoire*) is the main attraction here. Paintings, masks, sculptures, malachite jewelry and original works made out of copper and steel wire are for sale.

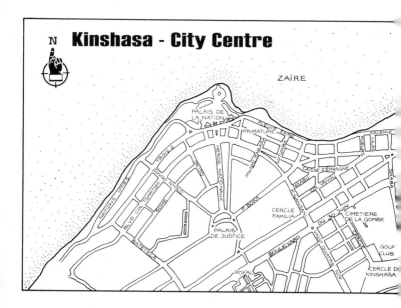

As mentioned before, the railway station is at the north end of the Boulevard. Across from it, though hardly recognizable, is the bus stop, from where buses run to Kikwit and Matadi. Finding your way in Kinshasa is relatively easy because all the streets run into the Boulevard at some point. There are enough buildings or spots which can serve as landmarks for meeting points. The tall, modern Sozacom (Société zairoise de commercialisation de minérais) building of a brownish brick colour is also a good landmark. Standing across from it is the ONATRA building (National Transport Office). The big supermarket Sedec is behind the Sozacom building, and further on is the Avenue des Aviateurs with the Galeries Présidentielles, where the boutiques determine the latest chic style in Kinshasa's world of fashion.

For those needing to retreat from the pell-mell of the Boulevard, there is always a quiet corner at the pool bar in Hotel Memling. The cafés Tutti-frutti and Chantilly are also good retreats for a welcome

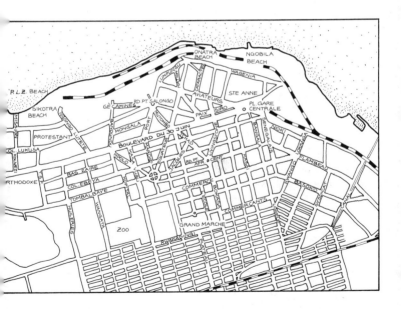

midday coffee or tea. Nevertheless, Gombe does not make up all of Kinshasa. Branching off to the right of the Boulevard into the avenue Kasa Vubu is the colourful, very African district La Cité, which extends south of the large market. A separate world with its own laws, in which more than two-thirds of Kinshasa's entire population lives. One really does not know if it is misery or just the way of life here. The living spaces are crowded into narrow alleys which turn into canals of mud after heavy rainfall. Many of the young people, who left their villages to look for their fortune in the metropolis, have exchanged a feasible subsistance way of life with one of uncertainty. Obviously the desire for material well-being and for the so-called modern lifestyle is stronger.

Wandering through the Cité late in the day when the sun is hanging like a glowing fireball between the alleys, and the glaring light changes movements into shadow plays, when smells and sounds are discerned as strange and foreign, one thinks once again, Africa is a mystery.

A visit to the **grand marché** is no less of an experience. The market here, like everywhere, is not only a place to exchange goods for money but also for news. It represents an important communication centre of the population. Likewise, this territory has its own rules, which are determined exclusively by the self-confident Mamas, who are in complete charge of family-life.

Further on is the Kasa Vubu which runs straight into another district, the most cheerful in Kinshasa, Matonge. The music prevails here, blaring round-the-clock from every nook and cranny. People are dancing in dusky bars (Ngandas), sitting or standing outside, chatting, drinking beer. One thing is certain, Matonge is not a caricature; the cheerful easy-going lifestyle here is authentic. A positive outlook on life is characteristic of Zairians everywhere, not just in Matonge. In this way article 15 *debrouillez-vous* (see to it that you manage) is applicable and effective, even when the situation appears hopeless.

Back again to the Boulevard: Its extension is the Avenue Colonel Mundjiba which leads to the Mont Ngaliema. The president's residence is located here, surrounded by a large park with impressive sculptures by Zairian artists. The zoo within the park attracts many visitors. Not far from here is the Cité de l'oua, an elegant village providing accommodation for visiting state officials.

Travelling farther south from the Mont Ngaliema on the road towards Matadi, one comes upon the Binza district, situated on top of a hill. Here, hidden behind high, protective walls, are the villas of high officials, ambassadors and wealthy citizens. Also located here is one of the most exclusive restaurants, La Devinière.

Ndjili Airport Kinshasa

The tourist or one travelling on business, arriving for the first time at the Ndjili airport Kinshasa, should for the time being forget accustomed standards.

As is the case in all airports in the country, there are no announcements by intercom, signs or tables for orientation (except those at the check-in counter). You will have to ask your way through or let yourself be swept along with the tide of people, whether it be upon arrival or departure. But take comfort; before you can turn around, the keen eye of an airport assistant (or whatever they prefer to call themselves) recognizes your insecurity immediately and comes to your rescue. They can be identified by their green jackets in the otherwise indistinguishable turmoil in the airports. It is a respectable business, but it is better to ask beforehand "combien?" (how much?) for the offered services. This also applies to the luggage carrier in the yellow uniform.

A European working in Kinshasa said: "I always let the dispatch details be taken care of for me and pay for it, in order to avoid the whole business." There is no obligation to accept services of this type. Incidentally, there appear to be efforts in process to improve the situation at the airports.

As you pass through various points, you may be asked for tips or *cadeaux*.

Arrival: It would be best to establish contact with a Zairian or someone familiar with the country on the flight to Zaire. They could be helpful for passing through customs, when claiming luggage and getting a taxi. It is possible that someone might offer to take you into the city centre (for which you should of course offer to share the costs).

Luggage carriers, assistants, taxi drivers and taxi middlemen often are obnoxious in offering their services during the luggage claiming process. Take your time with everything until you have picked up your luggage and are leaving the airport. Listen for the going rate and try to hook up with other passengers (where possible with natives who know the local fares).

As in airports everywhere in the world, it is advisable to exercise the proper care over your hand baggage and luggage. There is, however, a check-point at the exit controlling the numbers on your luggage tickets making sure that they are the same as the flight tickets.

Outside there are sufficient taxis at your disposal, which are identifiable by their yellow or wine-red colour. If not expressed otherwise, they take several people. Do not get into the taxi until the price has been agreed upon. There are no standard fares, the price is according to demand. The evening fares are substantially higher than day fares, occasionally doubled.

Departure: It is absolutely essential to confirm your flight with the airline three days before the departure date. This can be taken care of by telephone, but it is highly recommended to go to the travel agency in person.

It is recommended to confirm the departure time of international flights the day before. It is advisable for national flights, if possible, to confirm your flight a few hours before departure.

For international flights (and connecting flights Kinshasa-Lubumbashi and return flights to and from Europe), cancellations or date changes at short notice are rare. It is a different story with national flights. All too often it happens that flights, perhaps even a few hours previously confirmed, are suddenly cancelled at the airport. Reason: no fuel.

More often than not you will learn of the cancellation by chance. You can gather from the murmuring disturbance in the waiting crowd that it is probably the case. Do not expect to hear the next scheduled flight announced at the airport.

Only patience, calmness and good humour can help in such situations. There is nowhere to go to complain.

The wise traveller takes precautions. Shortly before leaving the hotel, he implies the possibility of his return in case of a cancellation. And as for a longer stay than planned, he is not at a loss for things to do since he left a few sights to see for such an occurence.

If the flight is on schedule, passengers gather in the semicircle part of the airport building two hours before departure. For international flights this is quite orderly, but for national flights there is lack of organization.

Tickets and passports are submitted at different desks. You have to wait until your name is called before you can check-in your luggage and have your ticket and passport returned. The departure area is to the right of the ticket hall. The passport check is here, and beyond that is where vaccination documents are controlled. It is important to carry your vaccination document with you for all national flights. It is often requested. Hand luggage is controlled after this.

When leaving the country, it is important to remember that you are not allowed to take with you Zairian money. So keep just enough zaires to buy a drink before you go.

Airlines
Air Zaire, 4, Avenue du Port, B.P. 8552, Gombe, tel. 24985, 24988, 23580, airport office, tel. 23660. City office open M-F 8.30-16.00, Sa 8.30 -12.00.
Air Zaire, 29/30 Old Burlington Street, London W1X 1LB, 071 434 1151/2

Accomodation
Hotels
- L'Afrique Hotel, 4106 Avenue Colonel Mondjiba, B.P. 1711, tel. 31902, 31911, Kitambo. With restaurant and bar.
- Hotel La Crèche, 3 Avenue Badjoko, Matonge. Restaurant, bar, roof terrace. Very loud, in the middle of Matonge, but well-kept and inexpensive. Quickly booked up.
- L'Estoril (3 star), 85 Avenue du Flambeau, B.P. 10686, Gombe, tel. 27790, 27049. With restaurant. Central.
- La Funa, 1434, Rue Charpentier, B.P. 10686, Limente. With restaurant. Parking available.

- Guest House (Sozag Hotel), 1991 Avenue du Flambeau, B.P. 9052 Barumbu, tel. 24259, 23490. With restaurant, bar, garden terrace, parking available. Central, well-kept, inexpensive.
- L'Hotel de la Gombe (4 star, Invest Hotel), Avenue du Haut Commandement & Kauka, B.P. 8697, tel. 32981, With restaurant.
- L'Intercontinental (5 star), Avenue des Batetela, B.P. 9535, tel. 27284, 27285, 27005, 27355, Telex 21212, Gombe, Restaurants, night club, conference halls, boutiques, swimming pool, tennis courts and parking.
- Le Memling (4 star), 5 Avenue de la République du Tchad, B.P. 68, Gombe, tel. 23260-23266, Telex 21654. Restaurants, bar, conference halls, swimming pool, boutiques, centrally located.
- La Motel de la N'sele (4 star), N'Sele (60 km north of Kinshasa). Tel. 27085, 27405, 27680, for reservations. Kinshasa: tel. 31614, 26480, 26488, telex 21570. Hotel of the M.P.R. party. Restaurant, bar, congress halls, large swimming pool, entertainment park, zoo.
- L'Okapi (4 star), Avenue de l'Okapi, B.P. 10581, Ngaliema, tel. 81444, 80222, 800200. Restaurant, bar, congress halls, boutiques, swimming pool, tennis courts, parking lot.
- Le Phenix (3 star), 4251, Avenue du Flambeau, Barumbu, tel. 26627. With restaurant and parking.
- Hotel de la Presse (4 star, Invest Hotel), Avenue Kabinda, B.P. 8697, Lingwala, Cité de la Voix du Zaire, tel. 28052, 24123, 27785, Telex, 20443, Restaurant, bar, congress halls, parking.

Food and Drink
Restaurants
- Any, 3, Avenue Bangala, Gombe, Chinese restaurant.
- L'Arcadia, 44 Avenue du Port, Gombe, tel. 23139, closed Sundays.
- Les Baguettes d'Or, C.C.I.Z., 2nd floor, Gombe, tel. 28741, closed Mondays.
- Le Big Steak, Boulevard du 30 Juin, near main post office, tel. 25321, closed Mondays.
- Le Caf'Conc, 13, Avenue de la Nation, B.P. 12448, Gombe, tel. 26132, 27138. French cuisine. High class, high prices. Closed Wednesdays.
- Chez André, La Delice, Avenue Colonel Ebeya (behind the Memling), good Greek cuisine. Garden terrace.
- Chez Nicola, 88 Avenue de la Justice, Gombe, tel. 30253. International and Italian cuisine. Expensive. Open evenings. Sundays closed.
- La Ciboulette, Avenue de l'Equateur, Gombe. Well kept. Good French cooking, reasonable prices. Sundays closed.

- Le Cocotier, 20 Place commerciale de Ma Campagne, Joli Parc. International cooking. Open evenings. Closed Tuesdays.
- Le Comme chez moi, Place commerciale de Liment. International cuisine.
- La Devinière, Avenue de la Divinière, Gombe, tel. 27790. High class, expensive.
- L'Etoile, Hotel Intercontinental, Avenue Batetela, Gombe, tel. 27284, 27895. French and international cuisine. Closed Sundays.
- L'Estoril, 85, Avenue du Flambeau, Gombe, tel. 27790. Portugese cooking.
- L'Etrier, Avenue Colonel Ebeya/Huileries, Gombe, tel. 22583. French food. High class, expensive, Sundays closed.
- Le grand Muraille, Avenue de l 'Hotel/Av. des Avaiteurs, tel. 26620. Chinese food.
- Le Grill, Kasa-Vubu, in front of Rond-point Victoire. European and Zairian foods.
- INZIA, 6, Avenue Cadeza, Gombe, tel. 30435. Good Zairian food. Only restaurant with meat specialities like antelope, monkey, boa and turtle, (also vegetarian dishes *Fou-fou*, *Saka-saka* etc.): Garden tarrace.
- Lolo La Crevette, 128 Avenue Colonel Mpia, Joli Park, tel. 80172, 80912. Speciality Cossa-cossa (large prawns). Open evenings.
- Le Mandarin, Boulevard du 30 Juin, Bldg. INSS, 7th floor, Gombe, tel. 22068, Good Chinese food.
- Mona Lisa, Avenue du Port, Gombe, tel. 24717.
- L'Orangeraie, Boulevard du 30 Juin, Gombe, tel. 25556. International food.
- Le Piccolo, Avenue de l'Equateur. Italian cuisine, good pizzas. Garden terrace.
- Le Pique-Nique, 42, Avenue du Commerce, tel. 22770, Good international and portugese food. Sundays closed.
- Le Relais, Boulevard du 30 Juin, Gombe, tel. 26574. International cooking, high prices.

Snack-Bars
- Affaire Etrangérs, Place de l'Indépéndance, Gombe. Closed Sundays.
- Le Colibri, Avenue Colonel Lukusa, Residence Inga, Gombe.
- Le Café de la Presse, 347, Avenue des Aviateurs, Gombe.
- New Bistro, Boulevard du 30 Juin, in brown high-rise Sozacom building, Gombe. Fondues, coffee, etc. Occasional music groups, jazz. Also organize boat trips on the Zaire with a picnic. Closed Sundays.

Salons de Thé / Cafés
- Le Chantilly, Avenue Col. Lukusa, B.P. 14097, Gombe, tel. 24625. Good coffee and cake, snacks, breakfast.
- Tutti-Frutti, Avenue de la Paix, Gombe, tel. 25689. Good coffee, large selection of ice cream specialties, breakfast. Well decorated in terrace style. Closed Mondays.
- Patissserie Nouvelle, Avenue de l Équateur, Gombe. Coffee and cake, sandwiches, omelettes. Closed Sundays.

Bars
- Etoile Bar, Hotel Intercontinental, Gombe. Closed Sundays.
- Paillote, Hotel Intercontinental, Gombe.
- Veranda Bar, Hotel Intercontinental, Gombe.
- Le Pimm's, Boulevard du 30 Juin, building de la 2ème République, Gombe. Closed Mondays.

Transport
Car Rentals
- Avis, Hotel Intercontinental, Avenue des Batetela Gombe B.P. 16198, tel. 28005, Telex 21012, Telefax 22850.
- Europcar, Boulevard du 30 Juin, building Mayumbe, B.P. 15543, Gombe, tel. 25966, Telex 21530.
- Hertz, 11, Avenue des Aviateurs, B.P. 2135, Gombe, tel. 23322, 24477, Telex 21191.

Generally, the following conditions are valid for renting a car:

* Possession of an international (or Zairian) driver's license.
* Minimum age of 25.
* Paying a security deposit (not necessary for credit card holders)
* Use of vehicle only within the city limits (otherwise with chauffeur).

Example of Cost: (Avis) Renault 4 TL, 6,700 zaires per day + 67 zaires per km. For a week with unlimited mileage 80,000 zaires, with chauffeur approximately 2,000 zaires per day, petrol paid by hirer.

The international driver's license is valid for one year and only for within Kinshasa. A national (Zairian) driver's license can be obtained at the regional police headquarters. Presentation of one's national driver's license and 2 passport photos are the only requirements.

Driving in Kinshasa

The speed limit in the city is 60 km/h. Give way to traffic coming from the right, unless indicated otherwise. Traffic is directed mostly by policemen at the busy intersections.

The driver should always have his papers with him (passport, international driver's license, papers for the car, as well as an insurance card). Police controls are not unusual. Legal problems can be avoided in such situations by carrying the necessary documents with you.

Keep your patience and remain calm (and polite), regardless of what the problem is, if the process should drag on somewhat. Whatever the case may be, the policeman has no right to demand money from you. At best, he can give you a ticket, which you must take to the police station and pay, with receipt in return.

A few important telephone numbers in case of an accident: Police tel. 22171 (ambulance brigade tel. 25013/15, 24331), Ambulance tel. 26711-16713 (Hôpital Mama Yemo), in addition, there are police headquarters in every district.

City Public Transportation

The city buses operate from 5.00-20.00. Sotraz and a few other bus companies control the buses. In addition, private firms, the so-called *fula-fula* (from full in English), are in operation.

Both the city buses and others, however, are full to capacity not only during the rush hour, but at all times of the day and therefore are hardly recommendable for tourists.

The taxi system in Kinshasa, as in other cities in Zaire, is a practical alternative. The yellow taxis circulate along the main streets of the city, you only have to stop one on the way and indicate your destination. If this is part of the taxi's route, you can climb in. In some cases you may need to transfer taxis in order to get to where you want to go.

The taxi fare is paid after the ride. The whole process is a quick one, so it is advisable to have your money ready. The fare is hardly more than the bus fare - for a ride within the city centre the price is fixed (50 zaires).

There are always several occupants in a taxi. If an individual taxi is desired or if you want to travel to part of the city farther away, ask the driver for a ride express and negotiate the fare with him. There are no meters in taxis.

Whereas the yellow taxis circulate in the streets (most of them on the Boulevard), there is also a taxi stand in front of the Hotel Memling (the taxis are ruby-coloured). They generally drive express routes.

Excursions Outside Kinshasa

Travel agencies offer cruises on the Zaire with a few hours sojourn on a sandbank in the middle of the river. **Promotours** for example:

10.00	departure from Utexco beach
12.00/12.30	arrival at a sandbank
12.30-13.30	traditional buffet with specialties
13.30-16.00	various activities: swimming, hiking, sun bathing, visiting the fishermen etc.
16.00	return to Kinshasa
17.30	arrival in Kinshasa

Price per person including the meal 8,500 zaires, 50% discount for children between 2-12 years.

Hanns Seidel Foundation

Well worth mentioning is a remarkable development project which offers self-help aid (similar to the Sarvodaya villages in Sri Lanka) and in no way represents the paternalism common to many third world development projects.

The Mbankana-Project makes a new start in Kinshasa possible for young, unemployed people who have left their villages to try their luck in the city.

The village Mbankana is east of Kinshasa on the way to Kikwit. The young people are first of all educated in agriculture. The Hanns Seidel Foundation, which operates the project in cooperation with Kinshasa, has made available a piece of land approximately 26,000 ha on the savanna covered high plateau. Since 1980, people have been settling here, and currently there are 8 villages. The agricultural products are then sold in Kinshasa. The proceeds are used to build facilities for the community such as schools, wells, infirmaries etc. and also to pay off debts. Presently, this program has provided 2,000 people with opportunities for a new way of life.

One of the brochures published by the Hanns Seidel Foundation, with many photos and drawings by the village inhabitants, gives insight into the developments of this "new life in Zaire" (the title of the brochure). The villages are open to visitors. For those who are interested, please contact:

Hanns Seidel Foundation, Director Gerhard Leicht, B.P. 10815, Kinshasa I, tel. 22552-28097, 24394-28624.

Tourist Office
Office National du Tourisme, Croisement des Avenue du 24 Novembre et des Orangers, B.P. 9502, Kinshasa 1, tel. 30022.

Travel Agencies
- Agetraf, 87, Avenue des Aviateurs, B.P. 8834, Gombe, tel. 26921. Mostly for plane reservations. Iata office.
- Amiza, 600, Avenue des Aviateurs, B.P. 7597, Gombe, tel. 24602, 24603, Telex 21019. Plane reservations, excursions to Kivu (National Park and gorilla visits) and Haut-Zaire (National Park de la Garamba).
- Promotours, Avenue Colonel Mondjiba, Gombe, tel. 31335. Excursions in Kinshasa, Muanda, and boat excursions on the Zaire.
- Zaire Containers Voyages, Corner of Avenue Lukusa/Avenue Bandundu, B.P. 8733, Gombe, tel. 23418, 26784, 28316, Telex 21586. Excursions in Kinshasa and surroundings, Muanda, Kisantu.
- Zaire Safari, 1287, Boulevard du 30 Juin, B.P. 15672, Gombe, tel. 22417, 25828, Telex 21692. Excursions especially Kivu (National Parks, gorilla visits), Haut-Zaire (Mont Hoyo, National Park de la Garamba).
- Zaire Travel Service, 11, Boulevard du 30 Juin, B.P. 15812, Gombe, tel. 23288, 24875, 23232, 25170. Mostly plane reservations.

Shopping
Supermarket
Sedec is the biggest supermarket in the centre of the city, located behind the Sozacom building, Avenue des Aviateur.

Markets

Le Grand marché is in the Cité, between the avenues du Commerce, Kasa-Vubu and Bokasa. On the big square and in the surrounding streets, partially under cover, partially in the open, everything from fruit, vegetables, meat, fish, to household items, clothes, and brightly coloured and patterned African material are sold here every morning.

The market is not specifically for tourists, rather it represents an important centre of commerce and communication for the inhabitants of Kinshasa and its surrounding areas. The prices are fixed but it is not at all uncommon to bargain. Taking pictures is for the most part unwelcome. Considerate behaviour is appropriate in all cases.

The *marché de l'ivoire*, the so-called ivory market, covers the square at the end of the Boulevard du 30 Juin, in front of the railway station. Ivory, however, is the least of what one sees there. Often the canine-teeth of hippos and cow bones are carved and sold as ivory. The pieces can hardly be distinguished from ivory and are just as beautiful. Hippos, incidentally, are not an endangered species.

Pharmacies

There is a large number of pharmacies, most of them in the district of Gombe, the city centre. The business hours are the same as those for stores. Pharmacies with the description Modern or Omnium carry homeopathic drugs. The pharmacy Grandes Pharmacies du Zaire has a 24-hour service and can be found at Place Commerciale de Ma Campagne, tel. 81363.

Post Office/Telegraphs

Main Post Office: Office National de Poste et Télécommunications du Zaire (ONPTZ), Boulevard du 30 Juin, B.P. 7070, Gombe, tel. 22876, Telex 21480.

There are counters on the second floor, entrance Boulevard du 30 Juin, and on the first floor, side entrance. Open: M-F 7.30-12.00, 13.00-17.30, Sat. 7.30-13.00.

The telephone and telegraph office is open 24 hours a day. To get there, take the stairs to the right of the hall with the counters. A guard sits at the staircase to take your passport, for which he gives you a receipt.   Your passport will be returned as you leave (see Mail/Telephone/Telex).

Banks
- Banque Commerciale Zairoise (B.C.Z.). Boulevard du 30 Juin, Gombe, tel. 26401-26407, Telex 21127, 21159, 21314.
- Banque du Peuple, Boulevard du 30 Juin, Gombe, tel. 25161-25165, Telex 21108, 21202, 21398.
- Barclay's Bank, 191, Avenue de l'Équateur, Gombe, tel. 22356, 22578, 22777, Telex 21113. At this bank you can have money transferred from abroad.
- Union Zairoise des Banques (U.Z.B.), Avenue des Aviateurs, Gombe, tel. 25801-25805, Telex 21026, 21268.

Culture and Entertainment
Theatres
Théâtre du Zoo, Avenue Kasa-Vubu Théâtre de Verdure, open-air theatre, Mont Ngaliema.

Cinemas
The two biggest cinemas are the Ciné-Paladium, Boulevard du 30 Juin, Gombe and Ciné-Palace, Avenue du Commerce, Gombe.

Museums
Musee National de Kinshasa, in the Academie des Beaux Arts, Avenue du 24 Novembre, Gombe. Large collection of masks, ceramics, jewellery etc. of various tribes and epochs.   Occasionally there are special exhibitions. Sales of art works and paintings. Open: M,W,Th,F,So 9.00-13.00, Sat. 10.00-12.00, closed on Tuesdays. Entrance fee: donation.

Musee Universitaire, prehistoric museum at the university of Kinshasa, Economics Department, Campus de l'Unikin, Mont Amba. Open: M-F 8-15.00, Sat. 8-12.00.

Art/Sculpture
The following Zairian artists are among the most famous: Lubaki, Chenge, Maringa, N'Damvu, Bela, *Pili-pili* and Mwenze- Kibwanga.

Sculpting is exceptional in Zaire. Impressive sculptures can be seen in the park of the president's residence as well as on the university campus. The most famous sculptors are: Liyolo - his studio and gallery are located in Kinshasa, Mont Ngafula, and you can visit if you call beforehand (tel. 27798) - Tamba, Nzuzi, Mukendi, Nginamau, Mankana and Lufwa. The sculpture The Tom-Tom Drummer is one of Lufwa's works. It is the landmark for the Fikin Fair.

For information regarding art in Kinshasa and elsewhere, ask in the National Museum, Academie des Beaux Arts.

Zoo/Botanical Garden
Avenue Kasa-Vubu, Gombe, open daily from 9.00-17.00.

Golf
18-hole course, Boulevard du 30 Juin, Gombe

Foire Internationale de Kinshasa (FIKIN)
FIKIN, one of Africa's most significant international fairs, began in 1969. Exhibitors from many areas: industry, art, agriculture, etc., participate. National exhibitions take place in the even numbered years, the international in the odd numbered. FIKIN is a public institution, directed by an administrative council and management committee. For more information: Commissariat Général de la FIKIN, Enceinte de la FIKIN à Limete, B.P. 1397, Kinshasa 1, tel. 77506, 77549, 78440, 78443, Telex: 23329.

Various Addresses
C.M.Z. (Compagnie Maritime Zairoise), Avenue des Aviateurs, B.P. 9496, Gombe, tel. 25156, 25816, Telex 21626. Shipping company.
ONATRA (Office National des Transports du Zaire), 177, Boulevard du 30 Juin, ONATRA Building, B.P. 98, Gombe, tel. 24761-769, 22421, Telex 21017. Ship transportation on rivers and lakes.
S.N.C.Z. (Societé Nationale des Chemins de Fer Zairois), Avenue du Port, SNCZ-building, 5th floor, B.P. 10597, Gombe, tel. 26810, 22707, 22621, 24533, Telex 21627, Railway.
Sotraz (Societé de Transport Zairois), Avenue Général Bobozo, Kingabwa, B.P. 8226, Kinshasa 1, tel. 24503, 78445, 78211. Bus company in and outside the city.
Snel (Societé Nationale d'Electricité), 2381, Avenue de la Justice, B.P. 500, Gombe, tel. 32100, 32137, 30548, 32686, Telex 21347. Permission to visit the Inga Project.

Département de l'Administration du Territoire et Décentralisation, Avenue Colonel Tshatshi (across from Banque du Zaire), B.P. 3898, Gombe, tel. 31147, 31643, 32202. Permission for the entrance to the mineral zone Kananga/Mbuji-Mayi.

OFIDA, Office des Douanes et Accises, Boulevard du 30 Juin/Avenue du 24 Novembre, B.P. 8248, Gombe, tel. 32884, Telex 21461. Customs office.

Office Allemand de Coopération Technique- GTZ,(Gesellschaft für Technische Zusammenarbeit), 21, Rue Ituri, B.P. 7555, Gombe, tel. 32057, 31585, Telex 21451. Development aid.

Gendarmerie Nationale et de la Commission Nationale de Prévention Tourière (C.N.P.R.), sise 4, Bd. Sendwe, B.P. 9987, Kalamu, Kinshasa 1. Among other things they issue national driver's licenses.

Gécamines Exploitation (Général des Carrières et de Mines), Boulevard du 30 Juin, Sozacom building, 4th floor, B.P. 8714, Gombe, tel. 22362, 22950, 36107, Telex 21207. Copper industry.

I.Z.C.N. (Institut Zairois pour la Conservation de la Nature), 13, Avenue des Cliniques (across from Clinque Kinoise), B.P. 868, Gombe, tel. 31401. I.Z.C.N. is responsible for the administration of national parks and nature conservation.

Contact, 1492, Avenue du Flambeau, B.P. 54, Gombe, tel. 24840, 26168, 26203, 28890, Telex 21376. Publisher's address of Contact-Guide Pratique du Zaire, a practical guide to Zaire, mostly with numerous addresses. Available at the newspaper stand in the Hotel Intercontinental, among others.

Hospitals
- Clinique de Ngaliena, Avenue des Clinques, B.P. 3089, Gombe, near the Hotel Intercontinental, tel. 30315, 30316, 31258, 30234, 31256. Considered the best clinic in Kinshasa.
- Clinque Kinoise, Avenue des Cliniques, B.P. 3074, Gombe, tel. 30224.
- Clinque Universitaire, Campus de l'Unikin, B.P. 123, tel. 30123.
- Zaire American Clinic, 1054, Avenue des Batetela, B.P. 699, Gombe.
- Hospital de Kitambo, Avenue de l'O.U.A., Kitambo, tel. 59972. Chinese therapy, acupuncture.

Embassies
Zaire Embassy, 26, Chesham Place, London SW1X 8HG.
British Embassy, 191, Avenue de l'Equateur, 5th floor, Kinshasa, Gombe, B.P. 8049.

SOUTH OF KINSHASA

The Kinois' favourite place to visit is Le Joli Site, on Mont Ngafula, about 30 km from Kinshasa, on the road to Matadi. It is a hotel complex with restaurant and swimming pool, with a beautiful view. Not too far from Joli Site is the Lac Ma Vallée. The small lake, in the middle of the country, is a refreshing oasis. Here it is inviting to swim, hike or simply *dolce far niente* with a drink underneath one of the pleasant straw roofs at the bar...

Botanical Garden of Kisantu

This famous Botanical Garden is located in Kisantu (also called Inkisi), 120 km from Kinshasa.

In 1900, Brother Justin Gillet (1866-1943) changed a fallow marshland into a garden of tropical plants, which he had collected from all over the world. Today a collection of 2,500 plants can be seen on this 225 ha piece of land.

Besides plants like vanilla, cinnamon, pepper, cloves, etc., fruits from various parts of the world grow here, for instance mangosteens (quite different from mangos), which came originally from Vietnam. Curiosities such as *Ficus bengalensis* (a type of fig tree from India with immense aerial roots growing down to the ground) and the giant bamboos from Java, can be seen and admired. Cactus and orchid enthusiasts will be delighted to discover many rare species here. The Botanical Garden has a herbarium with 5,000 species, a small museum and a library with 3,000 books, many from the previous century. A rich field for botanists!

The village, with its gardens, idyllic lakes and enchanting paths, is peaceful and quiet. It is not only a tourist attraction, but also serves as a nature conservatory and a field for scientific research. For the amateur gardener, there is a nursery selling plants. There is also a restaurant. The Botanical Garden is open daily. Admission: 100 zaires.

NORTH OF KINSHASA

The fishing village **Kinkolé** (40 km from Kinshasa) can be reached via the expressway from the airport. The village is above all known for the political demonstrations, which took place on a gigantic square in the town centre. The activities at the fish market across from it are, however, probably more interesting for a tourist.

The restaurant huts along the river bank are especially typical. Here you can eat grilled fish prepared the African way, with Chikuang, and talk with the fishermens' wives. The best time to go there is naturally in the mornings or evenings when the fishermen come home, and the fish is fresh.

Hidden behind the reeds, are charming paths along the river bank. Another way to enjoy and discover the village.

Twenty kilometres further on the expressway (60 km from Kinshasa) is the **Domaine présidentiel de la N'Sele**. The seat of the president, the impressive Pagoda, was built in 1970 by Chinese architects. On these grounds is also a park, which extends to the river bank and borders the immense territory of the 4-star hotel complex N'Sele. The entire complex maintains a strict, cool, modern architectural style. The enormous conference rooms in the main building are utilized mainly for M.P.R. meetings. Accommodation is available for large groups in special wings as well as for families in bungalows.

Another attraction is the olympic-size swimming pool in the amusement park N'Selefolis. The peaceful, quaintly laid out zoo, with apes, wild boars, crocodiles, leopards and other animals, is a stark contrast to the amusement park. In the middle of the zoo is a place to buy drinks and a picnic area.

The toilets are also accessible to people not visiting the park for a small fee.

Also part of this domain is an estate, on the main road, with chicken and pig farming.

The expressway soon ends and continues as a tarred highway eastwards toward Kikwit. At the end of the path along the river is the idyllic village of **Maluku**, approximately 70 km from Kinshasa. Ever since the cozy hotel Grafura was built, with its terrace-restaurant, the village is among the Kinois' favourite weekend spots. Here one has a charming view across to the green slopes of the neighbouring country Congo. Visitors are led across by *pirogue*. The river's brown water is not particularly inviting for swimming.

Ask the fishermens' wives about Liboke and Chikuanga! Stools will be fetched instantly and the specialties served up...

TRAVELLING IN KIVU

The region of Kivu extends along the country's eastern border with Burundi, Rwanda and Uganda. The northern border of the *departement* runs a few kilometres from Beni, the western border near Kindu, and the southern near Kabambare.

The pearl of tourism, and certainly the most impressive and attractive landscape in Zaire can be reached from Kinshasa in just three hours flight several days of the week. Nevertheless, the distances in Zaire are immense. From Kinshasa to Goma is 2,600 km.

Kivu conjures at first thoughts of the Virunga National Park and its animals, the fishing village Vitshumbi, the bird paradise Ishango, Kahuzi-Biega National Park and the unique confrontation with mountain gorillas. The list of attractions goes on and on. In addition, there are the volcanic mountains, the *Route de la beauté*, the strange flora of the Ruwenzori Massif and the natural spectacles of the Rutshuru waterfalls and, overlapping Haut-Zaire, the Step of Venus.

An ideal climate, similar to that of the Mediterranean, prevails throughout the entire year. Due to the higher elevation of the Virunga and Mitumba massifs, the humidity is substantially lower than in the flat land and in the tropical rain forests. The rainy season and the dry season are not so strictly defined in Kivu. Except in July, it rains more or less throughout the entire year, mostly, however, only in short showers.

There is no shortage of good accommodation in Kivu, though the prices may seem a little steep.

Transport

Supposedly there is public transport between Goma and Butembo, at least twice a week. However, either the vehicles are *en panne*, (out of order), or the stretch is impassable due to mud. Ask at the Centre d'Accueil protestant (CAP) in Goma for information.

Certainly the excursions offered by the travel agencies in Goma or Bukavu provide the most comfortable way to travel in Kivu. This can be arranged beforehand in Kinshasa, whereby flight and hotel reservations and transfer from the airport are included. Among the agencies in Kinshasa (with offices in Goma or in Bukavu), the following specialize in excursions in Kivu including visits to the national parks: Amiza-Voyages, Zaire Safari and Kivu-Voyages.

If one wants to travel independently, yet fairly comfortably and in good time, renting a car with a driver is a possibility. This is, however, a question of cost.

The price of a rental car is fairly uniform. It is either a flat rate of about 210-250 zaires per kilometre with a minimum of 150 km a day, or a daily rate of 28,000 zaires. A smaller flat rate for the driver's travel expenses may be charged in addition.

Since the rental cars are actually mini-buses with seven seats, one could share with others. For this reason, you should consider finding a small group of companions at home (that does not mean that the group does everything together). Otherwise look for companions once you are Zaire.

The drivers know their way around and are generally very friendly and helpful. Furthermore, they practically take on the role of travel guide. They always manage to handle any given situation, even if the vehicle happens to be stuck in mud.

Especially during the peak travel season, it is exceedingly important to make reservations for the gorilla visit in Kahuzi-Biega or Djomba if you are travelling independently. This is also true for the animal safaris in the Rwindi section. Further information can be obtained at the IZCN Offices in Goma, Bukavu or Kinshasa.

The conditions of the roads play a fundamental role in Kivu. During the rainy season, some stages along the way can develop into downright mud battles. Once you are dug out of the mud, doesn't mean you are

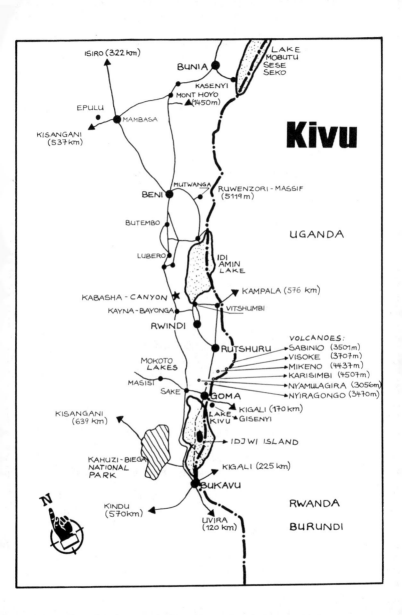

Kivu

ISIRO (322 km)

BUNIA

LAKE MOBUTU SESE SEKO

KASENYI

MONT HOYO (1450m)

EPULU

MAMBASA

KISANGANI (537 km)

MUTWANGA

BENI

RUWENZORI - MASSIF (5119 m)

BUTEMBO

UGANDA

LUBERO

IDI AMIN LAKE

KABASHA - CANYON

KAMPALA (576 km)

KAYNA - BAYONGA

VITSHUMBI

RWINDI

RUTSHURU

VOLCANOES:

MOKOTO LAKES

SABINIO (3501m)

VISOKE (3707m)

MIKENO (4437m)

MASISI

SAKE

KARISIMBI (4507m)

GOMA

NYAMULAGIRA (3056m)

NYIRAGONGO (3470m)

KISANGANI (639 km)

KIGALI (170 km)

LAKE KIVU

GISENYI

IDJWI ISLAND

KAHUZI - BIEGA NATIONAL PARK

KIGALI (225 km)

BUKAVU

N

KINDU (570km)

UVIRA (120 km)

RWANDA

BURUNDI

home free. Progress may be once again hindered by another vehicle stuck further along the way, (the driver may even have left his vehicle long before). For this reason, stretches, for example north of Luberos, are impassable. Then it is a question of waiting (but for how long?) or taking a *petit porteur* (airplane). To be on the safe side, travel during the dry season.

Another possibility is air travel through Kivu in stages. In addition to the airline Scibe Airlift, the small companies V.A.C. and T.M.K. Commuter also operate in Kivu. The small planes, however, are rapidly booked, therefore it is important to make reservations early.

Another adventure is a boat tour on Lake Kivu, from Boma to Bukavu or vice versa.

Examples from the Amiza-Program
Tour I: Virunga National Park

Day 1:

Arrival in Goma with Air Zaire. Reception at airport and transfer to Hotel Karibu for lunch. Subsequent departure by mini-bus to Virunga National Park. Stops at the Rutshuru Waterfalls and the Mai ya Moto hot springs.
Dinner and accommodation in Hotel de la Rwindi.

Day 2:

Animal safari lasting the entire day in Virunga National Park on the Kibirizi, Muhaha and Rwindi paths.

Day 3:

All-day animal safari on the Rutshuru path and visit to the fishing village Vitshumbi (sampling of fish prepared over an open fire with *pili-pili*) as well as to the Kabasha Gorge. Lunch, dinner and overnight stay in Hotel de la Rwindi.

Day 4:

After breakfast return to Goma. Lunch at Hotel Karibu. Visit to Goma and surroundings in the afternoon (lava fields, Green Lake, Sake Bay, Mont Goma etc.). Dinner and overnight in Hotel Karibu.

Day 5:   Free afternoon for shopping. Departure from Goma via Air Zaire.

Cost per person: individual US$ 1,282, 2 participants US$ 823, 3 participants US$ 669, 4 participants US$ 592.

Tour II: Virunga National Park and North Kivu

Day 1:   Arrival in Goma via Air Zaire. Reception at the airport and transfer to Hotel Karibu for lunch. Subsequent excursion by mini-bus to Virunga National Park. Stops at the Rutshuru Waterfalls and at the de la Rwindi hot springs. Dinner and accommodations at Hotel de la Rwindi.

Day 2:   Animal safari in the Virunga National Park on the paths Kibirizi, Muhaha and Rwindi. Lunch, dinner and accommodation at Hotel de la Rwindi.

Day 3:   All-day animal safari on the Rutshuru path to the fishing village Vitshumbi (try the grilled fish with *pili-pili*), and on the Ishasha path to Lake Kizi. Picnic at the lake. Dinner and accomodation in hotel.

Day 4:   In the morning, final hike in the Virunga National Park, optional. After lunch, continued tour on the *Route de la beauté*, through the Kabasha Gorge and via Lubero. Dinner and accomodation in Butembo at Kikyo Hotel.

Day 5:   After breakfast departure to Beni and Mont Hoyo. In the late afternoon,

groups of three accompany hunters from Balese into the forest and simulate an antelope hunt.
Dinner and accomodation in the Auberge du Mont Hoyo.

Day 6:   Morning excursion with a *pirogue* on the Loya River in the midst of the Equatorial Forest. Visit to the village Balese in the afternoon and opportunity to participate in the ritual dancing. Dinner and accommodation in the Auberge du Mont Hoyo.

Day 7:   Afternoon visit to the Steps of Venus and the grottos. After lunch departure to Butembo. Dinner and accomodation in Butembo at Kikyo Hotel.

Day 8:   Departure to Rwindi following breakfast. Lunch in Rwindi. Continued tour to Goma in the afternoon. Dinner and accommodation in Karibu Hotel.

Day 9:   Morning sightseeing in Goma and of the Lava Fields. Excursion to Mont Goma and visit to the Corniche (a road built into the rock wall). After lunch, to the airport and return to Kinshasa (Air Zaire).

Cost per person: individual US$ 2,627, 2 participants US$ 1,661, 3 participants US& 1,338, 4 participants US$ 1,117.

Tour IV: Virunga National Park and Gorilla Safari

Day 1-4:   identical to Tour I.

Day 5:   Departure to Bukavu by ship, *Vedette CVL*, crossing Lake Kivu (approximately 6 hours). Transfer to Hotel Residence in Bukavu, dinner and accommodation.

Day 6:	All-day safari in Kahuzi-Biega National Park. Visit to the bamboo forest to see the impressive mountain gorillas in the wild. Picnic in the park. Dinner and accommodation in the Hotel Residence.
Day 7:	After breakfast, transfer to the airport for return to Kinshasa via Air Zaire .

Cost per person: individual US$ 2,081, 2 participants US$ 1,429, 3 participants US$ 1,211, 4 participants US$ 1,103. Further discounts up to 6 people. Prices do not include the return flight Kinshasa-Goma or Bukavu.

Flight Connections in Kivu
Kinshasa-Goma and return 5 times weekly via Air Zaire and 3 times weekly via Scibe Airlift. Price (rounded-off) one-way: 49,000 zaires

Goma-Bukavu several times daily	T.M.C., V.A.C., Scibe
Goma-Butembo 4 times weekly	T.M.C. and V.A.C.
Goma-Beni direct, daily except Sat	T.M.C., V.A.C., Scibe
Goma-Bunia direct, once a week	Scibe
Goma-Butembo-Bunia, twice a week	T.M.C.
Butembo-Beni, twice a week	V.A.C.
Beni-Bunia, once a week	V.A.C.
(return on same day)	
Goma-Kalemie-Lubumbashi, twice a week	Scibe Airlift
Goma-Bunia-Kinangani, once a week	Scibe Airlift

GOMA

Goma (population 100,000) is situated at an elevation of 1,500 m at the foot of a volcano in the Virunga Massif. It is the most important region in Zaire for tourism. The airport in Goma has been extended for international flights. Avenue Président Mobutu runs a straight path through the centre of the city, stretching from one roundabout to the other. Shops and agencies of all kinds line the arcades on both sides of the avenue. At the southern roundabout is the main post office, a green building of classical architecture, which serves as a good marker. Further down the avenue and in the side streets are banks and hotels.

The northern end of Avenue Président Mobutu branches off to the left past the Zairian-African hospital and continues towards Bukavu. About 4 km from the city centre on this same stretch is Hotel Karibu, built in a pavilion style, located in a pleasant area.

There is an abundance of hotels in Goma, from the cheapest corner to the very comfortable. Goma not only represents an ideal starting-point for excursions and safaris, but it also offers relaxation for those needing a rest.

Located on the road on the way to the airport are a few boutiques and souvenir shops which attract many customers.

Whereas the centre of the city displays a colonial character, the outskirts have their own style of architecture, only to be found in Goma. The wooden huts are painted anthracite-black, similar to the ground of black lava. The only contrast to this rather dreary tone are the occasional yellow or green painted doors and window frames.

The bays of Lake Kivu appear to be reserved for the fishermen and the washerwomen. The tourist's search for a swimming beach is in vain. One can, however, cross over to Rwanda and indulge in the sun at Gisenyi's beach. A visa is not necessary, but there is a fee for cars.

Recommended is a climb up Mont Goma (a road leads up), located in the western part of the city, from where there is a good view of the city, the lake and the volcanic mountains.

Continuing north, travelling straight along the dirt road, beyond Avenue Président Mobutu, one comes to a picturesque residential area and market-place. The market is worth a visit.

Weaving through the maze of covered stands which line the narrow alleys, where women sit weaving baskets, one comes to the open market-place. Day in and day out, the market women sit on small hills of layered lava stone with their goods for sale spread out before them, dried pieces of manioc root, bananas, sugar cane, coal etc. It is a closed society, and a foreigner's every move is carefully watched by the rulers of this territory! Even the most inconspicuous attempt to pull a camera out of one's pocket will be immediately frustrated by a wild waving of arms.

Granted, this is Goma, and not a village somewhere deep in the jungle into which a stranger could have strayed. Nevertheless, here is a piece of homogeneous Africa! This is a place where the need for authenticity is given free expression. What business does a tourist have here anyway? If enticed to go there - and most people are - the tourist could simply change to buyer and purchase something from the goods displayed. With a visibly purchased item, he can go about his business undisturbed and casually capture a few African impressions with his camera along the way.

Hotels
- Hotel Karibu, B.P. 266, Northwestern edge of the city on the lake. Approximately 4 km from the centre. Pavilion style, restaurant, bar, swimming pool, tennis courts. Rooms with bath/WC from zaires 8,000.
- Masques Hotel, B.P. 530, 540. Centre, near main post office. Restaurant, bar, garden terrace. Exotic garden, swimmingpool. Sale of art objects. Rooms with bath/WC from zaires 7,000.
- Hotel des Grands Lacs, B.P. 253, Avenue Président Mobuto. Near main post office. Restaurant, bar. Rooms with bath/WC from zaires 5,000.
- Rif Hotel, B.P. 576, Rue Mont Goma, 320. Centre, restaurant, bar. Inexpensive, clean hotel. Rooms with bath/WC from zaires 4,000.
- Hotel Mont Goma, B.P. 320, 559. Centre, near main post office. No restaurant. Bar. Rooms with shower/WC from zaires 3,000.

For the low budget
Centre d'Accueil Protestant (evangelical Mission), Avenue Bougainvillea. West of the Rond-point de la Poste. Single room with shower and WC from 1,500 zaires (no admission after 22 hours).

Restaurants
- Hotel Masque, good international cuisine.
- Hotel Karibu, good international cuisine, music in the evenings.
- Hotel Grands Lacs.
- Taverne Restaurant, at the Rond Point de la Poste.
In addition there are many small African restaurants.

Travel agencies
- Amiza, Avenue Prés. Mobutu. B.P. 372, tel. 514. Excursions, car-rentals, flight reservations.

- Kivu Voyage Liwali, next to the Office National du Tourisme, excursions, car-rentals, flight reservations.
- Zaire Safari and Zaire Gorilla Safari, in the Masque Hotel, excursions
- Agetraf, Avenue Prés. Mobutu.

Tourist Information Office
- Office National du Tourisme (ONT), BP 730, Goma (near post office).
- IZCN, Institut Zairois pour la Conservation de la Nature, Avenue Prés. Mobutu. Information and reservations for the gorilla observation in Jomba and Kahuzi-Biega.

Banks
Banque Commerciale Zairoise and Banque de Kinshasa.

Drug stores
Several, for instance in the Avenue Président Mobutu.

Post offices
Main post office at the Rond-point de la Poste, green building Air Zaire, Avenue Président Mobutu.

Souvenir shops
- Galerie, Avenue de l'Aeroport. On the left upon entering the city from the airport. Jewellery, sculptures (old and new), batiks, post cards, etc.
- Caritas, at the Rond-point, mainly basket and pottery.

Camera shop
Pincha-Colour, Avenue Président Mobutu.

Ships to Bukavu
Vedette - every Sunday. Departure from Goma 7.30, duration approximately 6 hrs., return on Saturdays Bukavu-Goma, one-way fare: 1,550 zaires. The large ship *Karisimbi*, mainly used for cargo, runs daily. Departure from Goma 7.30, arrival in Bukavu around 18 hours. Fare: one-way 650 zaires. Reservations not necessary, fare paid on the ship.

Excursions from Goma
Climbing to the top of the Nyragongo and Nyamulagira Volcanos
The **Nyragongo** at an elevation of 3,470 m was last active in 1977. The climb is possible in one day. One can plan a 2-day trip and spend the

night in one of the huts on the way. Camping equipment is your own responsibility. Kibati is 13 km from Goma on the way to Rutshuru. The station is situated at an elevation of 1,950 m. Guides are available there. It is obligatory to have a guide for the climbing expedition. The climb takes 3-4 hour, the descent 2-4 hours.

To climb the 3,056 m high **Nyamulagira**, one needs two days. 1981 was the last time the volcano was active. The point of departure is 35 km from Goma, on the same stretch as mentioned above. Likewise, a guide is obligatory for the climbing expedition.

The travel agencies in Goma also organize climbing expeditions.

The Green Lake (Lac Vert)
A few kilometres from the centre of Goma, on the way to Bukavu, is this idyllic green lake. The surface of the water reflects the green slopes surrounding the lake.

The Mokoto Lakes
Further on the stretch to Bukavu, turning right before reaching Sake, are the Mokoto lakes, about 100 km from Goma. These four lakes are surrounded by breath-taking mountain scenery.

MASISI

One does not go to Masisi in order to experience the typical African way of life. Masisi gives the impression, rather, of a mountain landscape in Switzerland.

Upon leaving Goma travelling northwest, 27 km down the road towards Bukavu, turn right in the village Sake. A sand road curves its way into the higher mountain region. Only in dry weather is it a negotiable path for a mini-bus. It would be better to take a 4-wheel drive vehicle. The stretch is above all very muddy in the rains, moreover there is the danger of the automobile sliding off the path.

By planning the excursion for a Friday, one has the opportunity to visit the Marché du Mushaka (Mushaka = description of the region) on the way. Animals, for instance cattle, pigs , sheep and goats, in addition to vegetables and agricultural products from the mountain region are marketed here. A few more delays - it is often necessary to shoo away cows from the road - and after 60 km from Goma at an elevation of over 2000 m one finally reaches Masisi.

Here equatorial Africa is far away. Cows graze, a scene not disimilar to our part of the world. The humid tropical heat has given way to a cool, dry climate. It is spring throughout the year in Masisi.

Several farmsteads, specializing in cattle raising and horse breeding or dairy farms, producing butter, cheese, yoghurt, etc., are scattered throughout the region and are open to visitors. One should also take a look at the the mountain farmers' gardens. Vegetables and fruits grow here potatoes, celery, carrots, peas, strawberries, and also the mountain papaya, (different from large papaya), from which jam is made.

In addition to the Ferme de Lushebere (visit to cheese factory, accommodation available), operated by the Catholic mission, and the Ferme de Bunyole (visit to cheese factory, admission fee), the Ferme de Rushengo is specially set up for tourism.

The quaint, Chalet style house, also known as Auberge de Monts Verts, is situated at an elevation of 2,600 m, 65 km from Goma. The duration of the drive is approximately 2½ hours. The rooms are cheerful with a shower and WC on every floor. (Accommodation for up to 12 people). On several occasions the lounge provides a cozy evening atmosphere with logs crackling in the open fireplace. There is a video recorder and a small library as well. In addition, nine Arab horses are available at no cost to the house-guests for daytime rides (with or without escort). Other visitors must pay a fee for the horses. The area is also ideal for mountain hikers.

Accommodation in the Auberge de Monts Verts cost 5,000 zaires per person with full-board. To make reservations: Cit. Kulage, Wapatalea House, B.P. 429, Goma - or at the travel agency in Goma (or upon arrival if you are lucky).

From Goma to Bukavu

Often only the stretch north of Goma to Beni is called the *Route de la beauté*, however, the almost 200 km long section from Goma to Bukavu deserves this title as well.

The road, running along the western side of Lake Kivu, is generally negotiable even in the rain. One moment it winds around the idyllic bays of this lake, next it climbs the heights of the Mitumba mountain chain, which extends from Shaba to Kivu. One travels through typical African villages of clay houses, for whose inhabitants, a car driving by appears to be the attraction of the day!

First a view towards green valleys, then of the lake, where one catches a glimpse of a fisherman's *pirogue*. Lake Kivu does not yield much anymore. The waters have been polluted with methane gas.

Banana plantations are to be seen all along the road, and closer to Bukavu, grow coffee and cinchona. At about the half-way point is the mountain pass (1,980 m). The tiny African restaurants in the village of Nyabibwe are hardly prepared for tourists. It would be better to stock up on provisions in Goma for the trip (lasting approximately 4 hours). Occasionally along the way, you can buy bananas.

There is no bus between Bukavu and Goma. However, the following alternatives for the trip are:

1. rental-car from Goma
2. ride with someone else going that way - it is best to start looking around early for opportunities in Goma
3. by ship, whether it be the *Vedette*, the passenger ship running on weekends, or with the daily cargo ship
4. by air - there are several connections daily
5. or one can book an excursion with one of the travel agencies in Goma, together with a visit to the gorillas.

BUKAVU

The capital city of Kivu, (population 185,000) lies at the southern end of Lake Kivu at an elevation of 1,500 m. The city is built on several spits of land, pushes up the slopes of the massif and appears to want to extend even further.

New residential areas, whose rectangular mud huts with corrugated sheet iron roofs joined together in a charming terrace-style, seem to grow out of the brownish-red soil like weeds. Tea plantations and cinchona are imbedded in the slopes of the mountains between forests of pine and eucalyptus. From the bark of cinchona, which comes originally from Peru, quinine is extracted. The quinine is processed at the local plant Pharmakina.

The city itself does not offer much with respect to attractions; rather, it is the periphery which is of interest to a visitor.

The Avenue Président Mobutu, lined on both sides with stores, hotels, banks and agencies, is the main artery of the city, although not terribly busy. Buildings connected with arcades are witness to the colonial period. The Residence Hotel is supposed to have once been the scene of important social happenings. The hotel looks as if it has seen better days.

Further from the Avenue Mobutu one comes to a narrow spit of land, upon which office buildings, residences and occasionally somewhat abandoned-looking villas are hidden in the green trees and vegetation. At the farthest end is a sports centre with facilities for water sports, tennis and table tennis. Far off on top of a hill, is the cathedral with its visible green dome.

Markets take place daily in the city districts Nyamugo and Tshimbunda. Tshimbunda is a picturesque residential area, very African, whose huts are built in terraces on the loamy soil of a cliff. During heavy rains, the streets lower down are inundated with mud, and often entire huts are washed away. Visitors may feel they should only venture into the labyrinth of narrow streets with the escort of a native, although a few friendly words and glances will quickly dispel any feeling of unease. In any case, from here and from way up on top, one has a splendid panoramic view of the city, Lake Kivu and across towards Rwanda.

A drive through the Ruzizi valley , on the stretch towards Burundi, is fascinating as well. One can visit the dam and hydroelectric power plant, which supplies South Kivu, Burundi and Rwanda with electricity.

The main attraction of Bukavu is without a doubt the Kahuzi-Biega National Park (30 km away) and the opportunity to observe the eastern lowland gorillas.

If the visit to the national park falls on a Sunday or Thursday, fanciers of typical African markets should be sure not to miss the market in Mudaka, on the way to the national park, about 15 km from Bukavu. A visit to this very colourful market would be better with the escort of a native Zairian. Taking pictures is not welcomed there.

Hotels
- Hotel Residence, Avenue Président Mobutu, B.P. 406, tel. 2941. Rooms wtih bath/WC from zaires 10,000. Bar restaurant.
- Hotel Riviera, Avenue du Lac. On the peninsula, directly on the lake. Rooms with bath/WC from zaires 6,000. Bar, restaurant, night club.
- Hotel Belle-Vue, Avenue Président Mobutu, 2266. Small, clean hotel, simple rooms with shower/WC from zaires 3,000.
- Hotel Metropole, Avenue Président Mobutu. Simple, but comfortable hotel. Rooms wth bath/WC from zaires 2,000. For the small budget!
- Hotel Fregatte, Avenue Président Mobutu. Simple Hotel. Nice inner garden. Rooms with bath/WC from zaires 3,000.

Restaurants
- Restaurant Bodega (belongs to Hotel Residence), Avenue Président Mobutu. Best restaurant here. Prices somewhat high but reasonable for the quality. International cuisine.
- Restaurant Hotel Riviera, Avenue du Lac.

There are also numerous simple restaurants available.

Travel Agents
- Amiza, Avenue Président Mobutu, B.P. 2836, tel. 2877/78, plane reservations, excursions (Kahuzu-Biega National Park).
- Agetraf, Avenue Président Mobutu.
- Cercle Sportif, on the peninsula. Bathing beach, boat rentals, water skiing, tennis, table tennis.
- Centre culturel français, 118, Avenue Président Mobutu

Bank
Union Zairoise de Banques. Banque commercial zairoise.

Post
Avenue Président Mobutu. Open M-F 7.30-12.30, 13-16.30, Sat. 7.30-12. Telecommunication, Avenue Président Mobutu (next to the post office).

Open 24 hours, also on Sundays and holidays. The main Post Office is outside the city, near the university.

Ships to Goma

Vedette- every Saturday, departure from Bukavu 7.30, about a 6-hour trip, one-way fare 1,550 zaires. The return trip Goma-Bukavu leaves every Sunday at 7.30.

Large ship *Karisimbi* daily. Departure Bukavu 7.30, arrival in Goma about 18 hours. One-way fare 650 zaires.

Reservations for trips not required. Payment on board.

Topic: Women

For those interested in the situation of Zairian women, the manager of the regional office for the organisation **La Condition feminine**, Citoyenne Bachu, will discuss the work and goals of this national relief organisation. It is mostly concerned with the life and working conditions of rural Zairian women. The office is in the Gouverneurs Building.

Address: Citoyenne Bachu Behati Nyenyezi, Secretaire Regional à la Condition Feminine et a la Familie au Sud-Kivu, B.P. 2514, Bukavu.

THE KAHUZI-BIEGA NATIONAL PARK

The Kahuzi-Biega National Park is located about 30 km from Bukavu on the way to Kisangani. It was founded in 1970 and covers an area of 600,000 ha. The park takes its name from the two highest peaks: the 3,308 m high Kahuzi and the 2,790 m high Biega. The region of thick mountainous forest was claimed as a national park primarily in order to protect the eastern lowland gorilla which is an endangered species.

The national park lies at an elevation ranging between 1,800 m and 3,300 m. The vegetation varies accordingly. The bamboo forests make up 37% of the entire park and lie between 2,400 and 2,600 m. Above 2,600 m the area is savanna covered with heather. Other animals live hidden in the thick forest, namely buffaloes, elephants and chimpanzees. The average temperature in this mountain region is about 16° C. The dry season is from June to August. Besides the gorilla observation (see next page), these excursions can be made in the national park:

National Parks

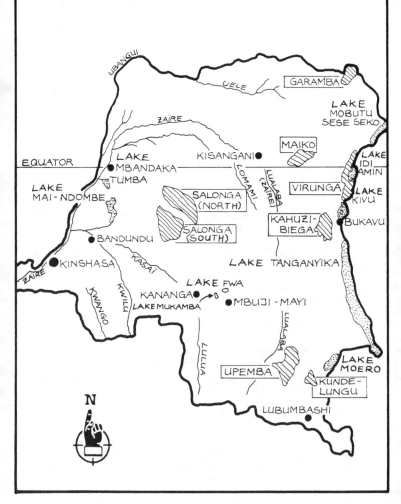

1. Climbing the 3,308 m high Kahuzi, the highest point of this massif, lasts approximately 3 hours. The path passes through rich Alpine flora, and from the summit, one has an extensive view of Bukavu and Lake Kivu. The descent takes about 2 hours. Rain coat and provisions should be taken along, and it is advisable to wear sturdy shoes or hiking boots.

2. Picnic on the Mont Bugulumiza. A 6 m long path leads to the summit. One can hike up the trail or take a cross-country vehicle. A splendid view from here to Rwanda and, on a clear day, as far as the Virunga National Park. Same equipment as excursion 1.

3. The road to Kahuzi-M'Bayo. This stretch leads to a tea plantation 20 km away from the national park. Here you can enjoy wonderful views over Lake Kivu.

The station Tshivanga in Kahuzi-Biega National Park lies at 2,050 m. There is an inn there which can sleep up to 12 people, shower and bathroom facilities available. Food must be brought with you. Approximately 10 km away there is a camping site. A cross-country vehicle is requisite for the journey.

There is no public transport between Bukavu and Kahuzi-Biega National Park. Taxis are available in Bukavu.

The Life of the Gorillas
Gorillas are classified into three well defined races:

1. The western lowland gorilla (*Gorilla gorilla gorilla*), which is found in Gabon and Cameroon.
2. The eastern lowland gorilla (*Gorilla gorilla graueri*), which lives solely in East Zaire, between the right-hand river bank of the Zaire and the eastern mountain range of the country (Maiko and Kahuzi-Biega National Parks),
3. The mountain gorilla (*Gorilla gorilla beringei*), which is native only in the mountain region of the Virunga-Massif (Zaire, Rwanda, Uganda).

In former times, the mountain gorillas lived at the foot of volcanos under 2,000 m but due to land exploitation have been driven to higher elevations (between 2,500 and 4,000 m). The entire stock was estimated at between 280 and 308 in 1986. They were grouped together in 29 families, with 12 lone gorillas.

The eastern lowland gorilla, which is often mistakenly called mountain gorilla, lives in Kahuzi-Biega National Park. According to a study from 1979, 223 gorillas (14 families and 5 independent) were estimated.

A family is comprised of 6 to 37 members. The leader is at least 15 years old and can reach a size of up to 180 cm and 200 kg. The patriarch of the family is not only recognizable due to its tremendous stature, but also because he has grey fur on his back, (silver-backed). The patriarch chooses his successor from the young, fertile males around 10 years old, the so-named black-backs. Only the silver-back is entitled to reproduce. The young males not selected to be part of this social structure remain either as **bachelors**, or they choose a female from another group and start their own family.

A gorilla family inhabits a territory of up to 30 km^2, which generally overlaps the territories of other families. Their life-span is estimated to be between 35 and 40 years. They are exclusively herbivorous. Leaves, liana, wild celery, fruit and the marrow of bamboo branches represent their main dietary intake, and feeding occupies most of the day. The insects consumed unintentionally provide a good source of minerals.

The Karisoke Research Station has been documenting the mountain gorillas since 1967. The founder, Dian Fossey, who, for 18 years, led studies on the mountain gorillas and lived among them most of the time, vehemently tried to protect the animals against poachers. It is suspected that they were responsible for her death in 1985.

Currently, there are two gorilla families in Kahuzi National Park, with the names Maheshe and Mushamuka, who are accustomed to the presence of people and have become approachable. The poacher also tries for months to approach the gorillas and win their trust through daily contact. He is mainly interested in the silver fur on their backs.

A scream from the patriarch, often confirmed with pounding on the chest, is his way of demonstrating his protective authority or is a

manifestation of his demand for respect. They can intercommunicate with a wide range of vocalizations and gestures.

Changes in the way the habituated animals live is not yet evident, though a small increase in live births has been recorded.

The Kahuzi-Biega Park, like all other national parks, is administered by the Institut Zairois pour la Conservation de la Nature (IZCN). The project in Kahuzi-Biega is a joint Zairian and German effort, in cooperation with the GTZ (Gesellschaft für Technische Zusammen-arbeit - an association for cooperation in technology).

Observations of Mountain Gorillas

The excursion to see the mountain gorillas is restricted to a maximum of eight people per day per gorilla family, in order not to alter their normal behaviour patterns. It is important to make reservations early at the IZCN (Institut Zairois pour la Conservation de la Nature) offices in Kinshasa, Goma or Bukavu. It is possible, especially during the peak tourist season, that the tours in Kahuzi-Biega and above all in Jomba are booked weeks beforehand. Tour groups from neighbouring countries, Uganda and Rwanda, often come to Jomba as well. Tours at short notice are possible at other times of the year, however; one must call the IZCN office beforehand.

The group is led by a tour guide and two others who free the path of undergrowth with their machetes and look for traces of the gorillas. The trekking through the forest is quite strenuous at times, therefore good physical condition is a must. It can take up to four hours before the gorillas are discovered.

As for clothes: most practical are long, cotton trousers or jeans, a long-sleeved shirt, sturdy trainers or, if available, hiking boots with good grip. Only old clothes and shoes should be worn. Furthermore, it is a good idea to carry a small backpack for camera, rain jacket, beverages, first aid, etc., in order to keep the hands free.

It is important to follow precisely the instructions given by the tour guide. He is very familiar with the behaviour of the gorillas because of his daily contact with them, and he knows how best to react in every situation. From footprints, recognizable as trodden down patches of earth, branches that have been chewed on, fresh excrement, and the gorillas' camp from the night before, the guide can determine the distance to the animals. When they are found you are able to observe the gorillas undisturbed in their natural habitat for about 45 minutes.

The visitor's fee is, for adults $100 (only US $ accepted), 50% discount for children. Children under 15 are not permitted. The price includes the tour guide and permission to take pictures; flash, however, is prohibited. (The guide and the path-clearers would be grateful for a tip nevertheless.)

The departure point for the guided tour is the entrance to the national park, Tshivanga.

A few recommendations: Appropriate behaviour during gorilla observations (published by IZCN/GTZ):

1. Remain with the group and always follow the guide.
2. In case the patriach approaches you, do not retreat. Follow the instructions of the guide.
3. By no means try to touch one of the young gorillas. This could cause a conflict with the head of the family.
4. Calm movements and keeping quiet are important.
5. During the observation, do not eat or smoke (danger of transmitting human diseases).
6. Do not leave anything behind (cigarette stubs, food, bottles, etc.). The gorillas collect litter and may eat it.

The Scream of the Maheshe
My confrontation with the mountain gorillas in the Kahuzi-Biega National Park

One morning, as I was waiting at the Tshivanga Station, the entrance to the Kahuzi-Biega National Park, (elevation over 2,000 m), I noticed a young chimpanzee lying in the shade fighting for its life. Emaciated and feeble, he kept scratching the wounds on his little body. A jerk, a slight raising of his eyes, then the heavy eyelids fell again, finally to sink into the sweet relief of sleep.

My attention, absorbed in this scene, was abruptly diverted by the sharp clicking of military boots and the ceremonial saluting of the park's small guard troop and their commander. The warm morning sun, a small group of people waiting, and now peace and quiet, as if everything had stopped. A few of the guards' wives, with babies strapped on their backs, were busy in front of their huts - an idyllic peaceful scene.

When the park director arrived, another formal salute took place, and immediately things came into motion at the Tshivanga Station. A group of three gathered together with the guide and path-clearers, they set off on their hike to one of the two gorilla families.

I had the opportunity to join three Frenchmen, employed in Zaire, who had arrived in their 4-wheel drive vehicle. Seven of us, including the tour guide and the two path-makers, got into the car. Our path led along a slope, lined with eucalyptus which offered splendid views of Lake Kivu with its many islands. Soon, we arrived at our destination, in the middle of a tea plantation, the starting point of our excursion to see the second family of mountain gorillas, the Maheshes.

A steep slope led up to the mountain forest. Our voices became more restrained as we followed each other single-file.

I couldn't see a path anymore, and my feet kept getting tangled up in liana and aerial roots. I grabbed these for support when I started slipping. I had to hold my arms above my head to shove my way through thorny bushes. I ducked like the person in front of me and crawled on all fours on the damp, moss-covered ground, only then to stumble over tree trunks or roots lying across the path. We hardly said a word to one another, and, for me.

Occasionally, I turned my attention away from the path and listened to the mysterious murmerings of the tropical forest. A collage of odours penetrated my nose; the fresh, bitter smell of shade-loving plants and the musty odour of the earth. The indescribable green of the forest enchanted me and looking up into the canopy of the forest I became disoriented. I no longer felt as if I was just me, but part of this great universe.

The short, hissing swings of the machetes brought me back to the scene. Often the clearers left the group to look for new paths if our way became impossible. Then we would be signaled to follow or they returned to explain the route. Meanwhile, two and a half hours had passed. Up to this point, our only traces of the gorillas have been a few meagre, dried up manure piles, which were not worth paying attention to.

Where was I? In which direction had we been walking? I had lost all sense of direction.

All of a sudden the guide pointed to a banana shrub flattened to the ground - the gorillas' previous nights camping site. That meant we couldn't be too much farther from them. From now on we must be really quiet, we heard from our tour guide, and he pointed to further signs of the gorillas - piles of fresh manure and broken off or nibbled branches.

My pulse quickened as if I were running a marathon. "Don't be afraid", were the final words from our guide. Suddenly I realized my complete dependency on him and utter trust and confidence in him. In silence we moved on together through the thicket; together only on the outside, individually each was wrapped up in his own universe of feelings and impressions.

Halt! Without saying a word, our guide pointed in the direction where the black, furry figure of a female gorilla was spotted in a clearing. Squatting in the thick growth with her baby at her chest, she nibbled away at the branches in apparent pure enjoyment. For a moment she penetrated us with her glance, then turned her attention and complete devotion back to her own business. We appeared to her as casual passers-by. My feverish exitement gave way to quiet, concentrated observing.

We become aware of another member of the family close by. Our guide signaled us to come closer. The body of the gorilla was hidden in a thick mass of grass and leaves, but his face: so near, so enormous and with such expression! I tried to catch his eye, and was hypnotized by the intensity of his gaze. I had the impression of communication between us, even a form of mutual understanding.

His glance was penetrating, but only lasting for a short moment, then he appeared not to be interested in us anymore. His attention was devoted to eating. Occasionally he looked up. I followed his every move with my eyes. With one quick manoeuvre he tore off a bamboo branch, pulled the bark off with his teeth and gnawed out the pith.

We stood as if frozen only 3 metres away, and could easily have taken pictures of the animals from further away.

All of sudden we were torn away from our quiet observing. Like a giant phantom, a gorilla of enormous size jumped out of the thicket into the clearing, only a few feet away! The silver-back.

He let out a piercing scream, which, as head of the family, secures him respect. Another scream followed, similar to the first one, but this time it was our guide in answer to the call. The massive gorilla lowered himself on all fours and made his way back into the thicket.

I stood there as if paralyzed. I asked him if such a situation could be dangerous. He shook his head: "Never. They are not aggressive animals, they're our friends."

Then we crawled into a dark, damp forest thicket, where more Maheshes family life was taking place: two balls of fur wrestled joyfully on the moss-covered earth, one moment rolling beside each other, the next on top of each other. Other family members appeared, taking notice of us but allowing us to continue observing, only to go back to swinging along the branches or to disappear again on all fours into the thicket.

The way back was shorter, and my thoughts revolved around what I had just experienced. What was so special about this wildlife exploration which set it apart from all the rest?

It was a genuine meeting! It wasn't man and beast standing so unbelievably close to one another, but two beings! And coming from the one, who appeared so wild, was an incredible, indescribable calmness and harmony.

And then there was the step by step approach, which gave me time to observe and experience nature to the fullest. Hadn't it also to do with the complete trust in our tour guide? Everyone has a different story to tell of their own individual experience. For me, it was a kind of a rediscovery of the lost paradise, or at least a notion of such.

From Goma to Rwindi

It is 130 km from Goma to Rwindi, to the station in the Virunga National Park. The road is passable even in the rainy season. From Goma on the road running past the airport, one drives through the blackened countryside due to lava from Nyragongo, which last erupted as recently as in 1977. Even early in the morning you will see many people on the road, taking their goods to one of the small produce markets or to the large market in Goma.

Almost always it is the women who carry the bulging sacks or overflowing baskets, banana bunches or canisters filled with *pompe* on their backs. Pompe, incidentally, is the term for the favourite local wine made from green bananas. Occasionally, bikes are used for transporting the market goods, or wooden scooters handbuilt by young boys. Often one sees young girls transporting heavy loads. They, like the boys, are called upon at a young age to take a fair share of responsibility in family affairs.

The road runs along the border with Rwanda, at the foot of the volcano Karisimbi. Running along the left-hand side is the Virunga National Park. The volcanic region is very fertile: corn, manioc, and avocados are cultivated. On the slopes grow peas and beans, and coffee plantations stretch across broad strips of land.

Just before reaching the village Rutshuru, there is a path leading to the Rutshuru Waterfall. Thick tropical vegetation frames the waterfall and the rising spray covers the plants like a silk web, through which the light dissipates in beautiful patterns.

The village of Rutshuru, named after the Rutshuru River which flows into the Nile, lies 73 km from Goma. Rutshuru is worth a short visit. It would be a good overnight station. The quaint hotel Grefamu has simple rooms at reasonable prices with showers and bathroom facilities as well.

It is another 55 km from Rutshuru to Rwindi. Just about half way is the entrance to the national park. The park entrance fee, however, is not paid here. The road through the park is the way to the north and to the fishing village of Vitshumbi.

Signs indicate that, from this point on, everyone must stay in the car. Baboons and gueraza cross the path, hippopotamuses can be spotted in the Rutshuru river or on the banks and in the undergrowth sometimes lions. On the right-hand side of the track, the simmering, sulphuric water of the **Mai ya Moto** springs bubbles up from the earth. Not too far from here is a sign pointing to the right, which leads to the fishing village of Vitshumbi (see *Vitshumbi*). A little further down the road is Hotel de la Rwindi and the Park Station.

The hotel's pavilions can be seen everywhere. It is a luxurious hotel with a restaurant, bar and swimming pool. The well-furnished rooms with shower and facilities, however, have a price: single room about $50.

Mountain Gorilla Observation in Jomba

Jomba is situated on the slopes of the 3,510 m high volcano Sabinio, not far from the border with Rwanda and Uganda. Two gorilla families are habituated to humans and are approachable. Jomba is approximately 90 km from Goma on the way to Rwindi. Not too far from Rutshuru, coming from Goma, the road branches off to the right. It is only about 20 km from this point to Jomba.

The Jomba station is situated on the top of a mountain slope and can only be reached by foot. The car is left behind at the foot of the mountain, and from there begins the steep ascent which lasts about a half hour. The entire duration for the trip from Goma including the hike up to the station is about three hours. One should plan to arrive at the station early, around 8.30. The excursion from here can be more difficult and strenuous than in Kahuzi-Biega, depending on how far away the gorilla family is located.

For more information and recommendations for the proper behaviour on the excursion, refer to the corresponding chapter for Kahuzi-Biega (*Observations of Mountain Gorillas*).

The visitor's fee, including the tour guide, is $100. It is to be paid at the station, and applications for admission must be settled previously at the IZCN office in Goma. Children under 15 are not permitted.

Camp de Jomba offers accommodations not far from the station. The chalet-style hotel is relatively new, first opened in 1988, and has quaintly decorated rooms, each with private facilities. Also in the hotel is a restaurant, a bar and terrace, and a video-room. The prices, however, are quite steep: per person $80, with full board $175. Simple accommodations at reasonable prices are also offered at the station.

Another possibility is the Grefamu Hotel in Rutshuru, 20 km away.

Zaire-Gorilla-Safari offers excursions to Jomba for $280 per person (for two participants). The price includes the trip from Goma, overnight accomodations with full board in the Camp de Jomba and the admission price to see the gorillas. Reservations are made at the Masque-Hotel in Goma or in the agency Zaire-Safari in Kinshasa.

A new station, Bukima, has been recently established, it is also in the volcanic mountains north of Goma. Another new addition on the stretch between Goma and Rwindi is the Tongo, where chimpanzees can be observed in the wild. Further information at the IZCN in Goma.

THE VIRUNGA NATIONAL PARK

Virunga National Park is the oldest, (established in 1929), and most famous of all the parks in Zaire. It stretches along the eastern border with Uganda and Rwanda. North of the park is Lake Mobutu-Sese-Seko, Lake Kivu lies at the southern end, and running through the middle of the park is Lake ex Edward (Lake Idi-Amin). The latter was once connected to Lake Kivu 15,000 years ago and became separated through a volcanic eruption.

Already in 1925 a section of the park was established for the protection of the mountain gorillas. The middle section Rwindi was added four years later and following that, the northern region Ishango and the Ruwenzori Massif. Today the park covers a total area of 800,000 ha. The Virunga National Park, along with Garamba and Kahuzi-Biega National Parks, was recorded in the list of World Cultural and Nature Inheritance by UNESCO.

Of Zaire's seven national parks, Virunga Park is the best developed. Tourism represents an important financial resource for the park, nevertheless the IZCN (Institut Zairois pour la Conservation de la Nature) must see to it that certain measures are carried out to protect the plant and animal life from possible negative effects of tourism. One of the main tasks of park supervision for all national parks is, however, directed against the practice of poaching. This appears to be an even greater danger than the influence of tourism.

Among the thorn bushes and cactus plants on the broad savanna and in the waters and forests live buffalo, various species of antelopes, hippopotamuses, elephants, lions, leopards, warthogs, hyenas, jackals, baboons, chimpanzees and a wonderful diversity of birds.

The largest known concentration of **hippopotamuses** is found in Zaire, an estimated 25,000. These animals may appear clumsy and lazy, but, despite their massiveness (up to three tons), they can run as fast as 45 km per hour. Hippos multiply rapidly; they have one offspring a year, and their life-expectancy is around 45 years. During the day one sees them dozing on the sand and river banks of the Rutshuru. In the river their backs protrude like miniature boulders. Part of their home territory is also Lake Idi-Amin. The lake has the hippos to thank for its abundance of fish - of the genus *Labeo* since they feed on the hippo's excrement (hippos mostly defaecate in the water).

A large concentration of **buffalo** is also present in Zaire (an estimated 15,000). They are gregarious, so one sees large herds. They too are herbivores and have a life-expectancy of 20-25 years. These dangerous animals can run a maximum of 55 km/hr.

The estimated number of **antelopes** in Zaire is 35,000. Many live as long as 20-25 years.

Elephants are particularly threatened by poachers, even to the point of extinction. There are an estimated 4,000 in Zaire. An elephant needs about 250 kg of plant food daily.

The **leopard**, being a nocturnal animal, is rarely seen, it is, incidentally, Zaire's national animal.

Virunga National Park is home to many reptiles. In Rwindi one finds guerazas, and in the Semliki River, the northern park region, crocodiles.

Here the botanist will find an inexhaustible and partially untouched region for study in the Ruwenzori Massif.

The park's reception office is located in a pavilion at the entrance to Hotel de la Rwindi. The office is open from 7 to 21 hours. Admission is $50 for adults and for children half-price. The price includes obligatory guide, permission to take pictures and is valid for several days.

Take your own car on safaris. Recommended visiting times: early mornings to noon or late afternoons. The animals seek shelter during the hot noon sun. In front of the reception office there is a chart where the animal observations of the day are listed.

The following tours are offered (more are planned):

1. Kibirizi track (26 km). Southwest of the hotel. Animals to be seen: herds of buffalo, antelopes, hippopotamuses, warthogs and occasionally lions.
2. Rwindi track (31 km). Along the Rwindi River. Same animals as the above mentioned, besides occasional elephants and, in a bay of Lake Idi-Amin, waterfowl.
3. Rutshuru track (48 km). This path has the most impressive landscape. The same animals can be seen here, especially large herds of hippos and more often lions.
4. Muhaha track (20 km). This leads to the fishing village of Vitshumbi among other places. Animal observation similar to 2.

The fishing village of Vitshumbi

The fishing village Vitshumbi is full of life and charm. It is located on the southern end of Lake ex Edward (Lake Idi-Amin), and, unlike the safaris, a visit does not require a guide. As previously mentioned, there are signs indicating the way to Vitshumbi within Virunga Park.

Animals and humans live in peaceful coexistence in Vitshumbi. The centre of village life is the fishermen's pier. Here the visitor finds himself in the middle of a merry, colourful spectacle. A flock of pelicans bob in between the painted fishing boats (*pirogues*) while the fishermen, market women and fish dealers are busy distributing their goods on shore. The pelicans, in their efforts to snatch a fish here and there, mix in with the confusion of people without the slightest hesitation.

Marabou storks parade through the village streets looking for something to eat. The villagers must guard their meals cooking in front of the huts on the fire. Otherwise the marabous help themselves.

Behind the pier the net menders are at work. A little further, around the spit, is where fish is dried. Not too far beyond is the pavilion where visitors can try the famous *tilapia* (fish), grilled on a wooden fire and spiced with *pili-pili*.

For further information on excursions in Virunga National Park see chapter Travelling in Kivu.

On the Route de la beauté to Mont Hoyo

Where does the *Route de la beauté* actually begin? For some in Rwindi, for others in Goma, and still others say that it already starts in Bukavu. In any case, the *Route de la beauté* goes to Beni.

From Bukavu to Beni it is approximately 550 km. Generally, both stages, from Bukavu to Goma and from Goma to Rwindi, can be driven during the rainy season. One, however, may have difficulties during the rains in the northern part, above all on the section between Lubero and Beni. If one wants to go this way and perhaps further north to Mont Hoyo, etc., it is advisable to inquire into the road conditions beforehand in Goma.

From the park station in Rwindi the road runs several kilometres further through broad savanna, then climbs up the Kabasha Gorge, soon to leave the edge of Virunga National Park.

At an elevation of approximately 2,000 meters, the *Route de la beauté* reaches **Kayna-Bayonga**, a village spread over several hills. Kayna-Bayonga is worth a stop. From the hill upon which the church is built is a good view of the entire village. Below that, on the road coming from Rwindi, is a small studio with masks and ivory carvings. There is one small, simple hotel on the main road in the village, Hotel Italy, with a restaurant. It is located on the village's through road.

From Kayna-Bayonga the road leads on past banana plantations, vegetable and cereal fields and quiet mud hut villages. In between Lubero and Butembo, at an elevation of 2,200 m, there is a sign with a

reminder that this is the equator. However, one would almost think that it was the Swiss mountains.

The village **Butembo** stretches between coffee and tea plantations at an elevation of approximately 1,800 m. Butembo is about 300 km from Goma and offers overnight accommodation in Hotel Kikyo, which has a restaurant as well. From Goma or Bunia to Butembo there are regular flights.

The *Route de la Beauté* ends 55 km from Butembo in **Beni**. Here simple overnight accommodation is available and there are restaurants as well. Possible flight connections exist from here to Goma and Bunia.

The road to **Mutwanga**, another 45 km, branches off to the right in Beni. This is the starting point for the climb up the 5,119 m high **Ruwenzori**. To climb Africa's third highest mountain requires five to six days (3 days ascent, 1 day rest at the peak, 2 days descent). More information can be obtained in the Rwindi park station or in one of the IZCN offices in Goma or Kinshasa. Accommodation is available in Mutwanga at the **Auberge du Ruwenzori**, which also organizes the climbing and photography safaris. The road from Beni via Mutwanga goes over the border to Uganda.

At the foot of Ruwenzori is another road leading to **Ishango**, 50 km from Mutwanga, situated on the banks of Lake ex Edward (Lake Idi-Amin) and the Semliki River. This village is idyllic. An especially large collection of waterfowl, as well as hippos, buffalo, antelope, etc. Currently there is no direct connection by boat between Vitshumbi and Ishango, however one is planned.

From Beni to Bunia is approximately 200 km. In between are several **Pygmy** villages. In the past, the Pygmies were hardly ever seen by outsiders, but today the villages have become a tourist attraction. Even organized excursions, for example to the village of **Oysha**, are offered by travel agencies.

With the permission of the village chief and of course for a fee, several of the villagers will perform dances or other rituals or daily activities, for instance making poisonous arrows or simulating a hunt. In any case, it is important to be cautious and considerate when visiting the villages. Even though some of the spontaneity may be gone, these are still people's homes.

South of Bunia is Mont Hoyo, 1,450 m high with its famous waterfall, the steps of Venus, and grottos. On top of the mountain, at an elevation of about 1,200 m, there is a chalet-style hotel, Auberge du Mont Hoyo, with comfortable rooms and a restaurant.

In Bunia, about 100 km from Mont Hoyo, there are hotels, banks as well as a small airport with regular connections to various places.

In Komanda, (125 km north of Beni), at the same intersection where it turns right to Bunia, there is a road turning left to **Epulu**. The village, named after the Epulu River, is approximately 230 km from Bunia.

In Epulu there is a preserve for okapis, animals closely related to the giraffe and only found in Zaire. The reservation is open for visitors. There is overnight accommodation at the station.

Bandundu
Gungu, Sociocultural Festival
The festival is the result of private intiatives put into action in 1986. The main idea is to preserve cultural heritage and stress its importance. It is also an attempt to win tourist interest to the region.

Gungu lies in Bandundu, 676 km from Kinshasa and 157 km from Kikwit. The road from Kinshasa to Kikwit is paved, but beyond that it is laterite.

The Kwilu and Lulua regions, southeast of Kikwit, have maintained a rich tradition of ritual and mask dances, in which the **Pende**, **Tshokwe** and **Lunda** tribes are especially distinquished.

The festival takes place every year in May or June and lasts several days. In 1988 for instance, 15 different tribes took part including the above with a total of about 3,000 people from five regions.

Dance contests between tribes and other performances are part of the programme. There is also a regional arts exhibition of ancient artifacts and modern art where one can make purchases. The opportunity to visit the sights of the Gungu region, the **Lukwila Gorge** and the **Kakobola** waterfall, are also offered.

Accommodation in Gungu is available in hotels of middle and lower price ranges. For more festival information or for reservations: Festival de Gungu, c/o Centre Culturel Français, B.P. 5236, Kinshasa X, tel. 25566.

HAUT ZAIRE: DE LA GARAMBA NATIONAL PARK

The 500,000 hectares of de la Garamba National Park are located in the northeastern region of Zaire, on the border with Sudan. The park was founded in 1938.

The savanna here is one of the last refuges for the East Africa race of the **white rhinoceros**. In addition there are lions, leopards, numerous antelope species, elephants, warthogs, and the now rare giraffe.

One of the park's special tourist attractions are the domesticated elephants at the Gangala-Na-Bodio station. Guided elephant rides are offered for $20.

The road to the park runs from Isiro past Dungu and further on in the direction towards the Sudanese border. From Dungu it is about another 75 km to the Gangala Na Bodio station. In Dungu and at the station there is overnight accommodation.

Several travel agencies in Kinshasa organize excursions to Garamba National Park. Details at the IZCN office in Kinshasa.

KISANGANI

Kisangani was once deemed to be the most beautiful city in Zaire. The city with a population of 370,000 lies in the middle of the equatorial forest. The English Africa explorer, Stanley (1841-1904), who followed the course of the Zaire River (then the Congo), first discovered the settlement in 1877, which, until 1966, was called Stanleyville.

Kisangani was victim of several extreme disturbances in the years following Zaire's independence between 1964 and 1967. Ruined houses and buildings stand as reminders of this period. The silent swaying palms loom over the pale rose masonry of a villa on Martyr Square knowing the secret story of past events. To be sure, these were once magnificent villas.

The city stetches on both sides of the Zaire. The railway station, with its line to **Ubundu**, 125 km away, is located on the west bank. This is, perhaps, the only reason that that side of the river would be of interest to the visitor.

Without question, Kisangani has its attractions. For example, the **Wagenia Fishery** which is famous for an unusual fishing method originating from an old tradition which is practised nowhere else in the world.

The fishermen have constructed a framework out of horizontal poles which are connected with lianas to wooden posts and placed in the middle of the rapids. Also attached by lianas are cone-shaped fishing baskets which are lowered into the water. The wooden construction is divided up into individual parts, each has two poles with a fishing basket in between. Each section is the property of one family and represents a considerable sum of wealth. It is passed down from generation to generation.

Twice a day, mornings at seven and evenings around five, the Wagenia fishermen sit on this wooden framework. The water flows calmly in the deeper water, and the fish swim against the current. At high tide they are swept into the baskets. The large-meshed nets, however, only catch the biggest fish, such as the *capitaine*. This method of fishing is not very profitable nowadays and is maintained only to preserve the tradition and attract tourists.

On the tiny islands on the river, not far from the wooden construction of the Wagenias, live the **Lokele fishermen,** who also practice an old fishing tradition. They fish with nets from *pirogues*. Often, for the visitor, they will dress in traditional garments as well.

The **Pêcheries Wagenia** is located approximately 6 km from the centre of the city on the road to Wani-Rukula. A fee is charged for the visit, explanation and photographing.

A visit to the Wagenia fishery can be combined with an excursion to another fishing village, **Wani-Rukula**, which lies 64 km from Kisangani. The drive is charming along the eastern bank of the river and through a section of the tropical rain forest, which in places gives an idea of its impenetrability. The road is paved the entire 148 km to Lubutu, although here and there it is in bad condition.

The inhabitants of Wani-Rukula appear to be used to occasional visitors. This is evident in the prices for the magnificent fish they pull out of their *pirogues* which are *à discuter*. Furthermore, they are not shy to demand a few zaires from an eager photographer.

The road stretches beyond Lubutu to Walikale and into Kivu, but until its completion it is recommended only for daring adventurers with 4-wheel drive.

In Kisangani it is more often the marginal things which attract visitors. The daily market in the centre is a play of colours. Around the market square are numerous shops underneath the arcades. Of particular interest are those which have a wide selection of typical African materials. Kisangani is known for its textile industry, Sotexki (Societé des textiles de Kisangani).

North of the city is a railway bridge over the Tshopo River which flows into the Zaire. Its waterfall is nearby and is well worth seeing. Upon crossing to the other side of the river one is once again surrounded by the luxuriant vegetation of the tropical forest. The simple, quiet life of people living there is closely bound to their environment.

Not far from the bridge turning left one comes to the Kisangani Zoo, not worth visiting, but a few feet beyond down on the bank of the Tshopo is a natural idyll. Once the **Bar des Zoo** attracted many visitors. Today it is an abandoned, solitary village, but nevertheless still beautiful. In the northern part of the city is the the third largest university in Zaire, (after Kinshasa and Lubumbashi).

On a late afternoon, as the sun slips over the dark relief of the tropical forest on the other side of the river, the road from the harbour to the restaurant **Yacht Club** is especially fascinating. At the piers where the *pirogues* dock there is normally the constant commotion of passengers being transported. At this hour, however, the bustle is stilled and the noise fades.

One can spend a quiet hour on the terrace of the Yacht Club Restaurant on the river bank. In the distance, the black silhouettes of individual *pirogues* interrupt the reflections of the setting sun on the water's surface. Several boats drift past the river's bank, in them the day's harvest, manioc or a good catch from the river. African scenes...

There are several direct flight connections a week from Kinshasa to Kisangani; one from Goma.

The ship *Courrier*, operated by ONATRA (Office National of Transport), runs between Kisangani and Kinshasa, but on a very irregular basis. This is unfortunate because the trip is quite an African travel adventure (see *ONATRA Harbour*).

The other ships in operation on the Zaire are for cargo. Often they will take individual passengers, so it is a good a idea to inquire about possibilities at the pier.

There is not a lack of hotels in Kisangani, but some appear to have suffered somewhat in their effort to adjust to the modern age.

Hotels
- Hotel Kisangani, Avenue Président Mobutu. Very simple furnishings; starting price 1,300 zaires.
- Hotel Olympia. Simple but orderly hotel, with restaurant, rooms with bath/WC starting at 2,000 zaires. In the hotel's inner courtyard is a small camping site which is frequented by those travelling across country by truck (organized trips from the U.K. or France).
- Hotel Wagenia, Avenue Général Mulamba, tel. 3497. Very simple furnishings, restaurant, rooms with bath/WC starting at 2,000 zaires.
- Hotel Zaire Palace, 12, Avenue de l'Eglise, B.P. 2052, tel. 2664. Restaurant, bar. Simple, neat rooms with bath/WC starting at 4,500 zaires, apartments starting at 10,000 zaires.
- Hotel Zongia, 4, Quartier des Musiciens, B.P. 2483, tel. 2265. Bar but no restaurant. Clean, quiet hotel with a friendly ambience, rooms with bath/WC starting at 4,000 zaires, apartments starting at 7,500 zaires.

- Hotel du Fleuve Beside the river near the *pirogue* pier, approximately 5-10 minutes from the centre of the city. This is a newly constructed luxury class hotel complex with a wing with cheaper accommodation. Restaurant, bar, swimming pool and tennis.

Restaurants
- Le Jardin, with bar. Quaint inner courtyard. Good international cuisine.
- Pergola, 7, Boulevard Président Mobutu, international cuisine.
- Psystaria, 17, Boulevard Président Mobutu. Simple, small but typical restaurant with international and Zairian cuisine.
- Yacht Club, directly located on the river, approximately 20 minute walk to the centre. Good, international cuisine. Quaint terrace on the river.

Nightclubs
To name a few: Cristal, Jumbo and Alida.

Banks
- Banque de Kinshasa
- Banque du Peuple
- Banque Commerciale Zairoise
- Union Zairoise des Banques

Miscellaneous
ONATRA Harbour, on the River Zaire. Information and reservations for the routes between Kisangani-Kinshasa. The ship *Courrier* presently operates only about twice a month. The dates are not available beforehand. Inquire at ONATRA office in Kinshasa or in Kisangani. Variety of cabins from the simplest to luxury class (2 beds) at prices between 15,000-35,000 zaires (Kisangani-Kinshasa). Duration of trip approximately one week (upstream Kinshasa-Kisangani at least nine days). The trip is not recommended during the dry season due to low water and the danger of running aground on sandbanks (around Kisangani from December to March).

Travel Agency Amiza, Boulevard du 30 juin, B.P. 1503, tel. 2875. Organizes excursions, for example, to the Wagenia Pêcheries and Lokele fishermen, rides in the *pirogues*, local dancers (upon request and in larger groups). Car-rentals with chauffeur.

Air Zaire, 12, Avenue de l'Église, tel. 3475/3476.
Scibe Airlift, Boulevard du 30 Juin, next to Amiza.
SNCZ (rail), Agence Rive Droite, on the Rond-point du Canon. Information and tickets for the train Kisangani-Ubundu. This simple and old train runs daily in alternation, one day to, the next day back.
Railway station, on the western river bank.
Private clinic, Clinique du Canon.

KASAI

Kananga and Mbuji-Mayi

A special pass is required to enter the mineral zone Kananga/Mbuji-Mayi. The cost is 20,000 zaires (spring 1990) and is obtainable at the Département de l'Administration du Territoire et Décentralisation (see Kinshasa). It is questionable whether it is worth the expense. Neither city has much to offer the tourist, although the two lakes between Kananga and Mbuji-Mayi, Lake Mukamba and Lake Fwa, are worth a visit. It is too bad that one cannot do this without the special pass.

The high plateau of **Kasai** is slightly hilly. The climate here is dry and warm, and even near the lakes there are few mosquitoes.

Kananga, the capital of West Kasai (Kasai Occidental), has 350,000 inhabitants. Large office buildings and commerce centres are prominent. The Lumumba Boulevard is the main street running through the city with hotels, travel agencies, restaurants and shops on both sides. Located in one of the large buildings is a small museum worth mentioning. Here, in a tiny space under scanty lighting, is an interesting exhibition of masks, ceramics and sculptures originating from various tribes. The guide here gives detailed explanations about the different objects. In the centre of the city there is a daily open market.

For those with a car there is a wonderful excursion to the **Katende Waterfall**, located about 20 km south of Kananga. The clear water of the Lulua River is good for swimming and fishing.

Occasionally the area is used for military manoeuvres. They build their camp off the path not far from the waterfall. If you encounter them you will have to ask permission to pass. A reminder that it is not permitted to take pictures of anything of a military nature.

The way to the waterfall goes past the modern American Missions Hospital which is open for visitors. The hospital has its own dam which generates a small electric power station.

Kananga is located 1,200 km from both Kinshasa and Lubumbashi. The road from Kinshasa is paved only as far as **Kikwit**; the rest of the way to Kananga is a sandy dirt road. From Kananga to Lubumbashi there is a connecting railway line, which continues to the north as far as Ilebo. Regular air travel exists from both Kananga and Mbuji-Mayi to Kinshasa.

The land is flatter around **Mbuji-Maji**, the diamond city with a population of 500,000. Mbuji-Maji is the capital of West Kasai (Kasai Oriental). Industrial diamonds are mined and processed here. This very hard mineral is utilized mainly for the manufacturing of tools. Visitors are led through the different process stages in the diamond industry, from mining to refining. The visitor's pass is free and available at the Société Minière de Bakwanga (MIBA) in Mbuji-Mayi.

The only possibility of travelling between Kananga and Mbuji-Mayi (200 km) is by truck. The sandy road is very rough and sometimes impassable, thus only recommendable in dry weather. More often than not the trucks get stuck in the mud. If a stop is not planned for Lake Mukamba, the middle-point, then calculate an entire day for the trip regardless of the point of departure. Take the first truck in the morning and take provisions along.

Lakes Mukamba and Fwa

Lake Mukamba is 180 hectares large and lies 109 km from Mbuji-Mayi and 90 km from Kananga. Trucks travel daily between the lake and both cities transporting people and goods. Other opportunities to take a lift may be available.

In addition, small planes with pilot are available in Kananga. More information concerning this is obtainable at the evangelical mission in Kananga. The landing strip is close to the CAP (Centre d'Accueil Protestant) on Lake Mukamba.

Lake Mukamba is a favourite vacation spot for the residents of Kananga and Mbuji-Mayis. Some even have a second home on the lake.

Tourism, however, still seems to be a foreign word. Especially during the week this is a quiet spot.

The only action to be found is in the Centre d'Accueil Protestant, the lodgings for the evangelical mission, when seminars or other meetings are being held. Tourists are also welcomed to stay at the centre. The tiny houses on the river bank belonging to the mission have rooms with one and more beds, a WC and running water. In the evenings, Mama, the wife of the centre's administrator, cooks *fou-fou* on an open fire and she is always glad when someone comes to keep her company.

This is an ideal area for relaxation, swimming and hiking. Demands for comfort, nevertheless, must be reduced considerably. The mission's lodgings are very simple; there are no hotels here.

Inquire in the CAP as to when and where a Village festival is taking place in the surrounding area. Even if there is nothing going on at the time it is interesting to visit the small, very typically African villages in the area and to chat with the villagers. The Chef du Village, the head of the village, will be glad to explain a little about the various customs.

Approximately 40 km from Mukamba is one of Zaire's most beautiful lakes, Lake Fwa. It is a deep lake with water as clear as glass. On the water's surface are colourful reflections of the surrounding vegetation mixed with the brown shades of the rocky ground. Swimming in the lake, however, is not recommended as it is infested with the trematode worm which causes bilharzia. Unfortunately one can only reach the lake if lucky enough to find someone travelling through.

The best way to get to Kananga from the CAP is to go to the intersection about 4 km away where trucks will usually stop. To reach Mbuji-Mayi in the other direction, wait at the main road, also not far from the CAP.

Hotels in Kananga
- Grand-Hotel, Boulevard Lumumba, tel. 2828, rooms with bath/WC starting price 4,000 zaires.
- Hotel Musube, Rue du Commerce. Simple, clean hotel which is often used as well by guests of the Catholic mission not far away. Rooms with running water starting at 2,000 zaires. Showers and WC on each floor.

- Hotel Canari, rooms with shower/WC starting price 3,000 zaires. Nightclub in the hotel, very loud.

Restaurants in Kananga
- Grill Art, Rue Lulua
- Taverne, Boulevard Lumumba
- Imprevue, Boulevard Lumumba
- Le Cercle
- Restaurant at the Grand-Hotel

Various **banks** are available in Kananga.

Air Zaire, Boulevard Lumumba

Restaurants in Mbuji-Mayi
Hotel Tanko, Avenue Cathédrale, bar, rooms with bath/WC.

Restaurants in Lac Mukamba
Centre d'Acceil Protestant (**CAP**), Lac Mukamba, overnight accommodation and meals around 2,000 zaires.

THE SHABA: LUBUMBASHI

Lubumbashi is Zaire's second largest city located at the southern tip of the country (660,000 inhabitants). The city stretches out over a savanna-covered high plateau at an elevation of 1,230 m. The border with Zambia is only about 30 km away. The climate here is comfortable with low humidity. During the dry season from May to September, however, it can get quite chilly.

Running through the city are broad streets lined on both sides with elegant and, in some cases, vacant villas. The streets give the city its spaciousness. A few interesting religious buildings can be visited in Lubumbashi: the St. Peter and Paul Cathedral, a mosque and a synagogue built in 1929.

The city as well as the entire region is dependent on the **copper industry** for its livelihood. Symbolic of Lumbumbashi is the huge mound of metal visible from the air long before the descent into the airport. **Shaba**, the name of the department, means copper in Kiswahili.

Even if Shaba (formerly Katanga) cannot compare with touristic Kivu, it has much to offer. The variety is what makes Lubumbashi and the surrounding area so interesting.

Surpassing everything are the various sports facilities the region offers. Famous far beyond the borders is the golf course in Lubumbashi where international tournaments are held.

In the city are several stud farms, tennis courts, a swimming pool (Hotel Sheraton-Karavia) as well as swimming lakes in the area, Lake Tshangalele near Likasi among others.

Due to the fact that Lubumbashi is Zaire's industrial centre, it is no surprise to find excellent restaurants and a 5-star hotel.

Art and culture are alive here. The names Bela, Pili-Pili, Mwenze Kipwanga and Kalumba are associated with Lubumbashi. Particularly interesting is a visit to the national museum (see page 97). The museum's interior design is very modern, but as one stands in the midst of the various tribal masks, sculptures and other objects pertaining to community and religious life, it gives a feeling of being transported into another world and another time.

The **Chenge** brothers are famous for copper reliefs and carved furniture. Their works are on display in their art gallery in Lubumbashi. Exhibitions of talented, young artists from all over Zaire are occasionally held in the Centre Culturel Français.

Also in Lubumbashi is a theatre. More information as to the city's current cultural and artistic events can be obtained at the Centre Culturel Français.

As previously mentioned, the copper industry dominates the city and is the country's main foreign currency earner. Other metals beside copper are mined in Shaba as well, for example cobalt, silver, lead, zinc and uranium.

A guided tour of the copper industry where the different stages of production can be observed is offered without charge. It is important to obtain authorization at the Gécamines office in Lubumbashi.

Lubumbashi, however, has more to offer than just golf and copper mines. Safaris, wild animals, wilderness, African villages, all of these things can be visited and admired. The national parks Kundelungu and Upemba are respectively approximately 150 km and 400 km away. Even the businessman is given the opportunity to enrich his trip with a contrasting safari in a cross-country vehicle, with tent and live-in cook, *cuisine à l'africaine*.

Hotels
- Hotel du Shaba, 3-star, 486, Avenue Mama Yemo, tel. 223617. Pleasant and clean, restaurant, rooms with running water and shower/WC starting price 4,000 zaires, individual bath/WC from 6,500 zaires.
- Park-Hotel, 4-star, Avenue Kasai, B.P. 112, tel. 223521-23, telex 41011, restaurant, rooms with bath/WC, single from 10,000 zaires, double from 14,000 zaires.
- Hotel Sheraton-Karavia, 5-star, Quartier Golf, B.P.4701, tel. 214512, telex 41049, telefax 225011. Approximately 4 km from city centre and 12 km from the airport. Restaurant, bar, swimming pool, tennis courts, boutiques. Rooms starting at 15,000 zaires.

Restaurants

Casa italien	-	Italian cuisine
St. Tropez	-	French cuisine
Beaulieu	-	international cuisine, expensive
La Grignotte	-	good quality, French and international cuisine
Versailles	-	good quality, Victorian style, international cuisine
Park Hotel	-	international cuisine
Lofoi	-	in the Sheraton-Karavia Hotel, international cuisine

Art/Culture
Musee National, Avenue Lubilashi. Interesting museum in newly designed rooms. Catacombs, masks, sculptures, ceramic pieces, etc. from different tribes are on display here. Exhibition of scenes from everyday life. Open: M, T, Th, F 9.00-12.00, 13.00-15.00, W 9.00-12-00, 13.00-17.00, Sat., Sun. 14.00-18.00. Admission and guided tour: donations welcome.

Chenge Gallery, Avenue Kimbangu. The Chenge brothers have made a name for themselves nationwide. Copper reliefs, oil paintings and carved furniture are on display. Open: M-F and Sun. 9.00-17.30, Sat. 9.00-12.00.

Centre Culturel Français, Avenue Mobutu. Occasional art exhibitions and other cultural events are organized by the institution.

Banks
- Banque Commerciale Zairoise
- Banque du Peuple
- Union Zairoise de Banques

Travel agency
Agetraf, Avenue Sendwe, B.P. 3672, tel. 222150, 222159, telex 41024

Car rentals
- Avis, Hotel Sheraton-Karavia, tel. 224515. Organize safaris as well.
- Europcar, Avenue Mam Yemo.

Riding stables
Information at the hotels or travel agency.

Copper industry
Gécamines (Générale des Carrières et de Mines), Avenue Kamaniola. Office open: M-F 7.30-12.00 and 13.30-16.00 (see below).

Open Market
Daily open market in the city centre, close to the railway station.

Zoo
Located at the city's western edge.

Bus routes
Several buses run daily from Lubumbashi to Kibushi, Likasi and Kolwezi. Direct departure from the market near the railway station.

Rail connections
Lubumbashi-Sakania (border to Zambia)
Lubumbashi-Likasi-Kolwezi-Dilolo (border to Angola)

Lubumbashi-Likasi-Kamina-Kabalo-Kalemie
Lubumbashi-Likasi-Kamina-Kabalo-Kongolo-Kasongo-Kindu
Lubumbashi-Likasi-Kamina-Kananga-Mweka-Ilebo

In addition to the slower trains, express trains with sleeping compartments and restaurant are available. Information and reservations at the station.

Tours of copper mines
The underground mines in Kibushi
Kibushi is 30 km west of Lubumbashi. Arrival by regular bus or taxi if the industrial tour has not already been booked as part of an excursion. The duration of the tour is approximately three hours.

Before entering the mine the visitor is fitted in miner's clothes and given a steel helmet and flashlight. The descent begins by elevator and continues in a truck taking you as deep as 1,300 m underground. The mine excursion is not recommended for those suffering from cardiac or circulatory disorders or claustrophobia since an interruption of the tour is almost impossible. In some areas the noise is intolerable and it becomes oppressively hot and sticky.

Open copper mine in Kolwezi and underground mines in Kamoto
Kolwezi is 406 km northwest of Lubumbashi. There are several regular buses travelling this stretch daily. Departure from the market in the centre of Lubumbashi. Hotels and restaurants as well as banks are here.

Copper factory in Lubumbashi
Tours of this copper refinery usually take place in the evenings. The colours of the liquid metal are especially impressive in the dark. More information and a tour permit are obtainable at Gécamines.

Caution: Taking pictures is not permitted in any of the facilities. Exceptions only with special authorization.

KUNDELUNGU NATIONAL PARK

The Kundelungu National Park is approximately 150 km north of Lubumbashi and covers a total area of 937,000 hectares. The park was established in 1970.

Antelope, warthog, hippopotamus, lion, leopard, zebra and baboon inhabit the broad steppes and thick forests of the Kundelungu mountain ridge. The best time to visit the park is during the dry season, from May to September. In the rainy season the animals flee the open steppes and seek refuge in the woods from the heavy rains.

A net of rivers and streams crisscross the park. The impressive **Lofoi Waterfall** is the highest waterfall in all of Africa, 384 meters. It is located 70 km from the Katwe station; a two hour drive from the station plus a 3 km hike.

The drive to the park leads through typical African villages. Quite striking are the rectangular mud huts, each imaginatively painted so that no two are alike. Some are decorated with carved pillars which support a porch roof. The most decorative hut, of course, belongs to the village leader.

Equally remarkable is the open and friendly atmosphere in the village. One could take a break and chat with the villagers. Incidentally, give the young boys your empty soda can (why not a full one?). These young artists make something useful out of everything - what better way to recycle?

A modest number of sleeping facilities are available in the park station **Katwe**. An alternative is to pitch a tent and bring along food and drinking water. It can get noticeably chilly in the dry season due to the high elevation (between 1,200 and 1,750 m), therefore it is a good idea to bring along warm clothing. Also advisable is insect repellent.

In spite of the patrols day and night, the poachers are still at work. If you are interested, let them show you the room at the Katwe station where they keep the confiscated poachers' weapons and traps.

The visitor's fee including guide: $20

As in Upemba Park, the fee is paid at the cashdesk. Neither park has public transport. The safaris offered by Avis are well organized, prerequisite, however, is four participants. Special arrangements can be made. For more information contact the Avis office in Lubumbashi or Kinshasa.

DE L'UPEMBA NATIONAL PARK

The de l'Upemba National Park was established in 1939. It covers approximately 1,000,000 hectares and is considered the richest of all reserves in Africa. Mainly the same animal species as in Kundelungu Park are found on the grassy savannas of de l'Upemba Park, and in addition there are many antelope species and a much larger concentration of zebras.

The Lualaba River (which flows into the Zaire) cuts through the northeast region of the park, likewise the Lufira, famous for its high waterfall. The lakes, rivers and swamp areas have a bountiful supply of fish and thus are a paradise for birds. The birdlife is a major contribution to the park's wide reputation. In addition to marabous, flamingos, cormorants and many species of ducks, there are predatory eagles and vultures.

There are two stations in the park: Kayo, about 350 km from Lubumbashi, and Lusinga, somewhat farther north. Both stations offer overnight accommodation.

Visitor's fee with tour guide: $20.

Worth mentioning here are the organized Avis safaris. In addition, small airplanes can land in Upemba Park. For more information contact Avis in Lubumbashi.

Examples of the Avis safaris with Air Zaire and Sheraton Karavia

Tour 1/1:	Safari in the Kundelungu National Park
Friday:	Departure from Kinshasa with Air Zaire. Arrival in Lubumbashi 2 hours later. Transfer to Sheraton-Karavia Hotel. Lunch in hotel, afternoon free. Departure to Gécamines at 18.30 for a tour of the copper factory. Return for dinner and overnight stay in hotel.
Saturday:	Breakfast in the hotel. Departure for Kundelungu Park at 7.30 by Landrover. Picnic at Katwe Camp (park station).

Ride through the park with the park supervisor. Dinner at the camp site (prepared by the cook). Overnight in tents (2 people per tent) or in the house.

Sunday: Breakfast in camp. Departure at 6.00 for **Lofoi**, the highest waterfall in Africa, approximately 70 km from the camp. Hike of about 6-7 km both ways. Return to Lubumbashi.

Monday: 5.30 to airport for departure to Kinshasa.

Tour 1/2:   Additional 2 days, 1 day longer in the park and a 1 day excursion to the copper mines in Kipushi with guided tour. Lunch in Kipushi. Dinner in the hotel. Return flight to Kinshasa on Wednesday.

Prices: Tour 1/1 BF 11,000 (Belgian francs) Tour 1/2 BF 17,000, flight not included for either tour.

Tour 2:   Sightseeing in Lubumbashi of the copper factory and Chenge studio and excursion to Lake Tshangalele (100 km to the north).

Tour 3:   Fishing-safari in Kinyama (150 km north of Lubumbashi).

Tour 4:   Safari in de l'Upemba National Park
Friday: Flight from Kinshasa. (see Tour 1)
Saturday: Breakfast in the hotel. Departure for national park at 6.00 by Landrover, distance approximately 400 km, mostly through bushland. Arrival at the camp site and setting up for evening meal and overnight stay (prices include meals during the trip).

Sunday:	Visit to the park. Lunch on the way. Return trip. Dinner in camp.
Monday/Tuesday:	View of the Kiubo Waterfalls on the way back to Lubumbashi. Arrival in Lubumbashi. Free dinner.
Wednesday:	Breakfast in the hotel. Departure to the airport for return flight to Kinshasa.
Price:	Tour 4: BF 18,000 (Belgian francs), flight not included. Trip to l'Upemba Park by airplane to join safari is a possibility; price upon inquiry.

Minimium participants: 4 people. Reservations in the Avis office in Kinshasa or Lubumbashi.

Tip: It is mportant to apply insect repellent before going on a safari and take it along with you. Also advisable are sun block, sun glasses and a hat.

TRAVELLING IN BAS-ZAIRE

By express rail from Kinshasa to Matadi

The trip by express train from Kinshasa to Matadi could be planned either at the start of one's trip as an introduction or at the end as a sort of 'summary' (see page 107 for schedule).

The trip is a rather sombre yet wonderful experience. During the seven hour trip the visitor experiences typical African scenes which remind him that he will always be an outsider.

The train departs from Kinshasa punctually, a good beginning for any visit to a new country. The traveller can sit back and forget about connections and delays, forget time, and is given the opportunity to adjust to this new world. Time and leisure are at one's disposal while sitting in one of the train's luxury compartments. What better opportunity to get into conversation with a fellow traveller and learn something about their country?

Perhaps, at first, a slight cautiousness is noticeable, but Zairians are generally very friendly and open-minded. Your questions will be answered with enthusiasm. You will not cease to be amazed, as the conversation leads to the theme of God and the world (if not here in the train, then at another time and another place), with what simplicity the Africans harmonize their mysterious ancestor worship and superstitions with the philosophy of the modern world. The African accepts both views and lives according to each of them. Nevertheless, the ancestors still have the final word...

Shortly before the Matadi train arrives, one or two others come into the station dropping off a flood of commuters. They disperse just as quickly as they arrived. The train departing from the Kinshasa station whistles promptly at 7.15. The luxury class is a compartment for 6 people with padded seats. Below the window is a tiny enamel sign reading "do not lean out".

The train is soon on its way, winding its way through the rich green, hilly landscape, arousing the villagers as it passes. As it stops at the larger stations, hectic activity is triggered off on the platform. Outside the window is a scene of bartering - the trip is a long one so it is a good idea to take advantage of the opportunity to buy a few chikwanges or bananas from the villagers although there is a dining car on the train serving soft drinks, beer and sandwiches.

The journey continues through a mango-paradise, whose fruit is just reachable from the compartment window, then the train passes through the rocky mountains of the Cristal Massif, whistling through the tunnels and winding its way through the narrow valleys, finally to arrive at the port Matadi on the banks of the Zaire River.

For an alternative return trip there are daily buses operating between Kinshasa and Matadi. It is recommended to buy a ticket to **Kisantu** - also called Inkisi after the Inkisi River. The village is 232 km from Matadi and 120 km from Kinshasa. The stop here is worthwhile.

The **Kisantu Botanical Garden** is famous and well worth a visit (see Kisantu Botanical Garden). Not too far northwest of Kisantu are the **Zongo Falls**, also quite an attraction. Simple overnight accommodation can be found in Kisantu. If you have the opportunity, look for a lift or

take a taxi 34 km to the **Mbanza-Ngungu** which is famous for its grottoes
where blind fish live. The caves are about 5 km from the village. There
are several hotels in the village, among them the luxurious Cosmopolite.

MATADI

Matadi has 16,500 inhabitants and is 352 km from Kinshasa. The
harbour is the main attraction. Trading vessels exporting agricultural
and industrial goods are Zaire's lifeline with the rest of the world. The
view of the harbour can be enjoyed but taking pictures is not allowed.

A visit to Matadi means a lot of climbing. The city is distributed over
several rocky hills on both sides of the Zaire River. The heat absorbed
and reflected by the rock is almost unbearable at times and causes a
certain lethargy. Nevertheless, Matadi is no less charming, and the
green taxis (operating under the same system as Kinshasa) will take the
tourist into every nook and cranny of the city very cheaply.

Take a drive up to the vantage point **Belvedère**. The harbour is to
the west; close to the impressive steel bridge, Pont Maréchal Mobutu,
stretching 722 m across the river Zaire. The bridge is relatively new,
built in 1983, and is one of Zaire's pride and joys. The road runs on the
west bank of the river, past Inga and Boma and to the Atlantic coast.

Distinguishable to the east are a section of the road and railway
tracks winding their way through the mountains and valleys. A relief
map at the viewpoint shows the course of the road, known as the
Chemin de Caravanes. In addition, there is an inscribed plaque in
commemoration of the workers who died either from epidemic or
exhaustion during construction of the Matadi-Kinshasa railway in the
last decade of the 19th century. The railway was opened 1898.

The colourful central daily market is also worth a visit. It is in the
lower part of the town to the west, terraced on the hill. On the other
side of the river behind the railway bridge is the road leading to Vivi, 5
km away. Vivi was Zaire's first capital in the days of the Democratic
Republic of Congo. There one can visit the museum of the explorer
Stanley. Upstream are the fishermen's caves of Kossa-Kossa with
inscriptions, dated 1487, cut in the rock by the Portuguese explorer,
Diego Cao.

A short way beyond that is one of the largest dams in Africa with its hydro-electric power station, the **Inga Project**, another pride and joy for the Zairians (see Inga).

Matadi has a considerable number of hotels, ranging from the simplest accommodation to the traditional **Metropole**. The hotel was built in 1930 in Venetian style, and upon seeing it, one can easily imagine the large social gatherings that formerly took place here. Incidentally, the hotels in Matadi are very good compared to those of the same class in other cities.

Hotels
- Hotel Metropole, 2, Rue Kinkanda, tel. 2638, 2639. Restaurant, bar. Room with bath/WC, air conditioning, single room starting price 4,000 zaires, double 6,000 zaires.
- Hotel Chez Tonton, Quartier Cine-Palace, B.P. 596, tel. 2207,2707. Restaurant with a small garden terrace. About 15 minute walk to the city centre (ville basse). Room with bath/WC, air conditioning, 1-2 pers. starting price 4,500 zaires.

Two star equivalent
- Hotel Munganga, 1104, Rue Kinkanda. Restaurant, bar.
- Hotel Kimin, Avenue Kinshasa.
- Hotel L'Embouchure, Avenue Kinshasa.
- Hotel M'bingu, Rue de la Plaine.
- Hotel Ciné-Palace, Avenue Président Mobutu.
- Hotel Mabilu, Quai du zaire.
- Hotel Kopway, Avenue Kinshasa.

Most of the hotels have restaurants, and small, African restaurants are located nearby.

Travel agent
Amiza, ville basse (lower part of the city), B.P. 264, tel. 2602, 2607.

Banks
Various banks in the ville basse.

Railway station
Approximately 10 min. from the centre (Hotel Metropole, ville basse).

City taxis

The green cabs travel around the city. City tour 50 zaires, further stretches, 1 passenger per cab, and express by arrangement.

Rail

Matadi-Kinshasa: Express train departure from Matadi: Tuesdays, Thursdays, Saturdays at 7 hours. Duration of trip approximately 7 hours according to the schedule.

Price one-way: luxury compartment (6 people) 2,020 zaires per person, open compartment 1,028 zaires.

Kinshasa-Matadi operates Mondays, Wednesdays and Fridays.

Bus

Matadi-Kinshasa: Buses of the companies Sotraz and Sitaz. Departure daily (including Sat. and Sun.) at 9.30 from the Sotraz bus stop. It is a good idea to get there at least half an hour early or to buy a ticket beforehand (ticket = seat reservation). Fare one-way: 1,800 zaires per person. Duration of trip according to the schedule, likewise 7 hours. A night-bus is also in operation departing Matadi around 22 hours. (Information obtainable in the Sotraz office at the bus stop.)

Bus/Minibus

Matadi-Boma: Minibuses, buses (Sotraz, Sitaz) and private taxis depart from the Rond-point. Regular departure times mornings around 7.00 and early afternoons between 14.00-15.00. The vehicles only depart when full. One-way fare: 800 zaires.

It is advisable to get there early to inquire on the spot about departure times.

Ship

Matadi-Banana (near Muanda): *Vedette*: Departing Tues. and Fri. at 8 hours. Duration of trip approximately 9 hours. (Return trip from Banana Wed. and Sat.) Fare one-way: 700 zaires per person.

Inga

Inga is an important name in Zaire. It is one of the largest dams in the world with a power station which, upon completion of the third stage of construction, will be the most powerful in Africa. The Inga Project plays a significant role in the industrial development of the country. The execution of the project is in three phases: Inga I, completed in 1972, 300 MW, production in 1986 = 541,620 MW. Inga II, completed in 1982, 1,500 MW, production 1986 = 2,487,550 MW. With the completion of the third phase, Inga III, the production will be doubled.

One can view the Inga-Project free of charge. However, it is necessary to obtain authorization at the Societé National d'Electricité (SNEL) in Kinshasa beforehand. From Matadi to Inga take transport enroute to Boma. Several travel agencies in Kinshasa organize excursions to Inga.

From Matadi to the coast

Zaire has a strip of coast only 40 km long. It may very well have been the Kinois' (inhabitants of Kinshasa) favourite vacationing spot at one time, but today the beaches appear rather deserted.

The two largest hotels on the coast near Muanda, Mangrove and Invest, appear to be operating in low gear, except, perhaps, during the peak season. The hotels just do not attract the guests like they used to! At one time the Mangrove Hotel had horses. Even if one does without the outrageously expensive motorboat rides, etc., the cost for both the hotels and restaurants are still very touristy.

From Matadi, Muanda and the coast are approximately 240 km away; from Kinshasa it is almost 600 km. One can cover the distance from Kinshasa in one leap with a plane. For a little sun and fun on the beach it is worth it.

More adventurous, yet also time consuming and more strenuous, is the trip by boat or over land. If one uses public transport the stretch is generally covered in three stages: Kinshasa-Matadi, Matadi-Boma and Boma-Muanda.

The road from Matadi to Boma is paved and well constructed. It runs through scenic, hilly landscape and passes the tropical forest Mayombe, which, extends into the Republic of Congo. What does it matter if you have to share your seat with another passenger - the beautiful scenery will quickly help you forget any discomforts!

The traditional arts of basket weaving, wood carving and sculpturing are still maintained in Bas-Zaire. On the way from Matadi to Boma you can see the craftsmen/women busily at work surrounded by their handicrafts on the side of the road. Even the cabinet makers can be seen sanding and hammering their bed-frames and cabinets outside.

Also typical for this region are the many small cemeteries along the side of the road. The graves are decorated with artistic tomb stones, and often lying on top are the tools or silverware which belonged to the deceased.

The road stretches further through peaceful settlements with open broad paths. The huts are mostly of red brick. On the deserted roads past the Mayombe Forest one sees the women in their typical bent posture carrying heavy baskets of firewood on their backs.

The trip from Matadi to Boma takes about two and a half hours (disregarding possible break-downs). If you leave Matadi early in the morning and, immediately upon arrival at the *rond-point* in Boma, catch a connection, you can reach the coast in another four hours. The road from Boma to the coast, however, is very rough and the marathon trip quite strenuous.

Boma was formerly the capital city of Belgian Congo until 1929 when the title was transferred to Leopoldville, (now called Kinshasa). The harbour city does not have much to offer in terms of sights, although the steel constructions of some of the colonial-style houses in the city centre are interesting. In the harbour vicinity, on the Quai du Zaire, not far from the Mabilu Hotel, is the famous Baobab connected with the Africa explorer Stanley. According to legend he spent his first night in Boma in the hollow of this tree trunk. For overnight accommodation Boma has simple class hotels.

The road from Boma to Muanda continues through flat land at the mouth of the Zaire River. Possible means of transport apart from private individuals are trucks which have been converted into buses. The seats, however, are very hard and the trip seems to last forever in these awkward vehicles. An alternative is to take the ship which operates Tuesdays and Fridays from Matadi via Boma to Banana (near Muanda). Information is obtainable in the harbours of Boma or Matadi.

Muanda is recognizable from afar by the flames from the natural gas refinery. In place of the red brick huts are grey, rectangular, one to two-storey houses on this flat, broad coastal land. From the centre of **Muanda** it is only 3 km to the sea. Walking along the coast to the north one comes to Hotel Mangrove, very rich in tradition with its rows of bungalows set into the rocky cliff. The Invest Hotel is only a few miles further with its bungalows situated in a bay good for swimming. Still further along the coast, about 14 km from Muanda, one reaches the fishing village **Nxiamfumu**, on the border with the Congo.

To the south, on the mouth of the Zaire River, is the small seaport Banana, where ships from Boma and Matadi berth. Overnight accommodation is available. One can get there from Muanda by taxi, a distance of only 10 km.

The daily market, spread out along the village streets and squares, seems to dominate the social scene in Muanda. Other social meeting places are the numerous bars located along the main road, especially on the road to Boma. Loud music blares from all sides of this miniature Matonge and may contribute to a less boring wait for those on their way to Boma. There are seldom any vehicles going to Boma, and it may be a while before the last bus-truck seat is filled so the trip can start.

You should count on scorching heat on the trip to the coast. It is advisable to double-check that your hotel room has functioning air conditioning or a fan.

Hotels in Boma
- Hotel Mabilu, Quai du Zaire, Harbour. With restaurant. Air conditioned rooms with shower/WC starting at 4,000 zaires.
- Hotel Excelsior, Avenue Maluku, in the harbour vicinity. With restaurant, bar, garden terrace. Simply furnished rooms, partially air conditioned, room with shower/WC from 4,000 zaires.
- Hotel Cine-Palace, Avenue Président Mobutu. Very simple furnishings, room with shower/WC from 3,000 zaires.

Hotels in Muanda
- Hotel Invest. On the coast, about 6 km from town centre. Restaurant, bar, swimming beach. Rooms (with and without air conditioning) with shower/WC from 10,000 zaires.

- Hotel Mangrove, Boulevard du 30 Juin. On the coast, about 4 km from town centre. Restaurant, bar, swimming pool, tennis courts. No swimming beach, rooms (with and without air conditioning) from 5,000 zaires. Organizes excursions.
- Hotel Mama Ekoko, Boulevard Président Mobutu, about 2 km from town centre and 1 km from the coast. Rooms (with and without air conditioning or fan) from 4,000 zaires. Restaurant. Inquire whether the generator and water are turned off during the night.

There are various **banks** in both Boma and Muanda.

TIPS FOR TOURS

Travelling in the country is dependent upon a number of factors, individual interests, time at hand, travel budget and delays along the way. For this reason it is not possible to make route suggestions with a detailed timetable.

At this point it should be stressed once again that discovering Zaire is only possible when you have a sufficient amount of time. Time in this sense means not only in terms of duration, but more importantly giving up all notion of time.

Of course you can get a brief impression of Zaire and a feeling for the country in two or three weeks of travel. If your interests are mainly in nature and observing the wildlife in Zaire, you should concentrate on Kivu. If this is the case, it would be best to book an onward flight to Goma immediately upon arriving in Kinshasa.

The following **Zaire at a glance** gives a quick outline of main travel destinations, in order of interest. Not all of the excursions can be embarked on from Kinshasa. Nature, landscape and typical African life as well as adventure is everywhere. (By adventure we mean the incidents on the way to your destination as well).

Be prepared for cancellations and delays and do not plan too tight a schedule for yourself with unalterable deadlines.

Zaire at a glance: Travel destinations
1. **Kivu**: Goma, Rwindi, Bukavu, Kahuzi-Biega or Jomba
    Interests: scenery, gorillas

Supplementary program:

a. *Route de la beauté* to Mont Hoyo
b. hiking (climbing the volcano Masisi, climbing Ruwenzori)
c. sports and relaxation (Hotel Karibu)

2. **Lubumbashi and surroundings**
    Interests: natural history, game animals (less than in Kivu), travel adventures (Avis safaris), copper industry, art/culture

Supplementary program:

a. sports (golf, tennis, riding)
b. relaxation (Hotel Sheraton-Karavia)

3. **Kisangani and surroundings**
    Interests: landscape, game animals, visits to African villages

Supplementary program:

a. river trip to Mbandaka (then to Kinshasa by air)
b. sports and relaxation (Hotel du Fleuve)

4. **Kananga/Mbuji-Mai and Lakes Mukamba and Fwa**
    Interests: natural history, scenery, swimming (few comforts), hiking, typical African villages, diamond industry

    At least a week is necessary in all the above areas. Those that follow can be enjoyed in less time.

5. **Gungu** (May/June)
    Interests: culture (cultural festival), scenery

6. **Kinshasa-Matadi Muanda and Boma on the coast**
    Interests: travelling by bus/rail, landscape, botanical garden, Inga Project

7. **Kinshasa**
    Interests: touring the city, open markets, art/culture, excursions to the surroundings.

Appendices

SHORT VOCABULARY IN KISWAHILI

to wake	kuamka	to stay overnight	kupanga
to pay	kulipa	to examine	kutezamia
to ask/request	kuomba	to forget	kusahau
to stay	kukaa	to sell	kuuza
to need	kuhitaji	to lose	kupoteza
to bring	kuleta	to do laundry	kufua nguo
tothink	kuwaza	to change/exchange	kugeuka
to eat	kula	to know	kujua
to experience/learn	kufundishwa	to want/wish	kutaka
to be missing	kukosa	to show	kuonyesha
to give (to somebody)	kupa	to be satisfied	kuwa razi
to go	kwenda	to come back	kurudi
to suffice	kutosha	1	-moja
to help	kusaidia	2	-wili
to buy	kununua	3	-tatu
to cook	kupika	4	-nne
to come	kuja	5	-tano
to make/do	kufanya	6	sita
to take along	kupeleka	7	saba
to like/love	kupenda	8	-nane
to be tired	kuchoka	9	kenda
must, have to	kuweza	10	kumi
to take	kutwa	50	makumi matano
to see	kuona	100	mia
to see/inspect/visit	kuangalia	Monday	siku ya kwanza
to be/become	kuwa	Tuesday	siku ya pili
to sleep	kulala	Wednesday	siku ya tatu
to cut	kukata	Thursday	siku ya nne
to write	kuandika	Friday	siku ya tano
to rest/relax	kupumzika	Saturday	siku ya sita
to sit down	kukaa kitako	Sunday	siku ya Mungu
to wash oneself	kunawa	week	juma
to look for/fetch	kutafuta	year	mwaka
to be drinkable	kunyweka	evening	magharibi
to drink	kunywa	morning	asubuhi

day/days	siku	family	jamaa
afternoon	mahana	child	mtoto
night	usiku	married woman	bibi
time	wakati	brother	ndugu
hour	saa	sister	dada
early	mapema	my name is...	naitwa...
yesterday	jana	What's your name?	
today	leo		Nawe unaitwaje?
tomorrow	kesho	I have	nina
since	tangu	you have	una
in a week	katika juma moja	he has	ana
a week ago	kuna siku saba	we have	tuna
village	kijiji	you (pl)/you (formal) have	mna
street/path	njia	they have	wana
turn-off/branch	panda la njia	I am at (place)	nipo
market	soko	you are	upo
money	feza	he is	yup
cheap	rahisi	we are	tupo
expensive	ghali	you (pl)/you (formal) are	mpo
which?	gani	they are	wapo
yes	ndiyo	Good day/hello	Jambo sana
no	hapana	How are you?	
each/every	kila		Hujambo (Hamjambo)?
there is/are	kuna	How is your husband (wife)?	
no, there is/are not	hapana		Bwana (bibi) hajambo?
to the village	mpaka mgini	What's new?	Habari gani?
until	mpaka	How are the children?	
I would like to	ningepende		Habari zwa watoto?
I would like	nataka	I'm doing fine	Si jambo
Thank you	akasanti sana	Good-bye	Kwa heri
please/you're welcome	tafazali	welcome	karibu
and	na	once	mara moja
also	pia	more	zaidi
together	pamoja	often	ara nyingi
just me/myself	peke yangu	much	Tele
it would be better	afazali	half	nusu
mother	mama	little	kidogo
father	baba	too much	mno
woman	mwanamke	very	sana
man	bwana	in, on	katika

where?	wapi?	shirt	shati
here	hapa	trousers	suruali
there	kule	dress	kanzu
near/close to	karibu na	shoes	kiatu
that is very far	ni mbali sana	doctor	doctor
bread	mkate	bed	kitanda
fruit	tunda	fever	homa
vegetables	mboga	heart	moyo
glass	bilauri	help	msaada
hunger	njaa	head	kichwa
knife	chetu	sick	mgonjwa
pepper	pilipili	hospital	hopitali
cooked rice	wali	nurse	mwuguzi
salt	chumvi	pains/problem	shida
sugar	sukari	pills	mbegu
plate	sahani	accident	msiba
table	meza	bandage	upapi
water	maji	wound	kikonda

I'm not feeling well; I have a headache.	Siwezi; kichwa kinaniuma.
I have been tired for a few days.	Tangu siku nyingi nimechoka sana.
Do you have a fever?	Una homa?
I don't know, I didn't take my temperature.	Sijui, sikupima homa.
I'm sweating a lot.	Anatoka jasho nyingi.
I'm feeling better now.	Sasa ninakuwa si jambo.

Taken from the "Guide de conversation - Swahili-Francais", C.E.L.A. in Bukavu, available in the Librairie St. Paul, Kinshasa (translated from French by Christa Mang).

SEWING A COTTON SLEEPING BAG

Material: (coloured) cotton material (4 m x 0,80 m), thread, 2 zippers
(each 50 cm long) or 4 drawstrings.

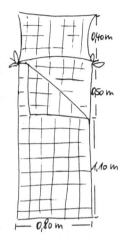

Put the material together as
follows: 1,60 m length doubled,
bottom piece 80 cm longer for
pillow section of which 40 cm are to
be turned under.   Sew seam on
upperside of sleeping bag and on
underside of pillow section.   Close
1,10 m side seams on sleeping bag
section.   Likewise close 40 cm on
side seams of pillow section (pillow
opening is on underside!).   Sew
zippers on each side of sleeping bag
section or leave a border for the use
of drawstrings.   (Measurements for
seams not calculated.)   A sweater or
pillow can be tucked in the pillow
section.

Index

Notes

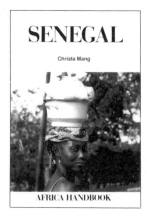

This travel guide gives helpful information for a different kind of holiday. Stay in rural villages amongst the people; experience the traditional festivals, tea ceremonies, unforgettable jungle taxi trips, the busy markets of Dakar and the Niokolo-Koba National Park. Travel routes and important sights are described as well as essential travel tips.

Bradt Publications
41 Nortoft Rd,
Chalfont St Peter,
Bucks
SL9 0LA
UK.

Hunter Publishing, Inc.
300 Raritan Center Parkway
NJ 08818
USA

ISBN 0 946983 54 2

ISBN 1 55650 308 3

AFRICA HANDBOOK

MALAWI

A. Hülsbömer
P. Belker

AFRICA HANDBOOK

In Malawi, the 'warm heart of Africa', you will find a wealth of new experiences. The loneliness of the wooded northern highlands, the challenge of climbing in the southern Mulanje mountains, the wonders of diving in the clear waters of Lake Malawi in the only freshwater national park in the world, and the excitement of trout fishing in Nyika Park. Follow the footsteps of David Livingstone and relive the first days of the mission set up in his memory.

You will be left with a memory of a sincere and joyful people, always ready to help the traveller.

Bradt Publications
41 Nortoft Rd,
Chalfont St Peter,
Bucks
SL9 0LA
UK.

Hunter Publishing, Inc.
300 Raritan Center Parkway
NJ 08818
USA

ISBN 0 946983 52 6

ISBN 1 55650 272 9

AFRICA HANDBOOK

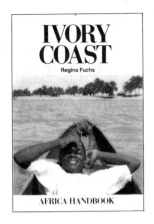

IVORY
COAST

Regina Fuchs

AFRICA HANDBOOK

The Ivory Coast has one of the most charming landscapes and is one of the most culturally interesting countries in West Africa. Wonderful untouched palm beaches, wide tracts of savanna grassland, unique crafts and a belief in progress and deep-rooted tradition are characteristic of the Côte d'Ivoire.

This handbook guides the visitor through this very foreign land, giving suggestions for day trips and tips on how to make a holiday here an unforgettable experience.

Bradt Publications
41 Nortoft Rd,
Chalfont St Peter,
Bucks
SL9 0LA
UK.

Hunter Publishing, Inc.
300 Raritan Center Parkway
NJ 08818
USA

ISBN 0 946983 53 4

ISBN 1 55650 279 6

AFRICA HANDBOOK